JESUS
IS MY
CEO

52 CHRIST-INSPIRED, PRACTICAL LESSONS
FOR ENTREPRENEURS

SIMON LEE

FREILING
PUBLISHING

Published by Freiling Publishing,
a division of Freiling Agency, LLC.
P.O. Box 1264
Warrenton, VA 20188

www.FreilingPublishing.com

Paperback ISBN: 978-1-956267-46-4
eBook ISBN: 978-1-956267-47-1

Printed in the United States of America

DEDICATION AND ACKNOWLEDGMENT

*To my late father who passed away in 2020 from cancer.
He supported me in every step of my life. From paying for all
my education to giving me the first check to start our business
in 2003, he was my biggest supporter and always had my back.
Dad, I miss you dearly. See you soon in heaven!*

*To my wife. In 2004, I started this company and also got married the
same year. I told her that I would not have salary for the next 3-4
years and we would have to live off of our savings. She responded by
saying, "I didn't marry you for your money; I married you because
of you." That gave me the biggest boost of encouragement to start this
company and to donate 50 percent of the profit away. Thank you to
my wife for always believing in me and cheering me on.*

*To all the men in my life who have helped shape who I am today:
Dr. Peter Swann, Pastor Andrew Gackle, Dr. David Daniels, Randy
Schroeder, and many others. Without the Godly men in my life,
I would not be here today. God used each one of those men to help
steer, exhort, and pray with me throughout a major part of my life.*

*Lastly, without Jesus, nothing would be possible. He saved
me when I was 16 years old. He gave me purpose in this life,
forgiveness of sin, and a future that is beyond my imagination.
To Him always be all the glory and praise!*

ENDORSEMENTS

"Five years ago, I launched a new kind of wealth management company to fulfill a vision God gave me. To make sure I was on the right track, I joined C12, a Christian peer-to-peer group full of other Christian CEOs. One of the first people I met when I walked into my first C12 meeting was Simon Lee. Few people forget their first meeting with Simon! He is a bigger-than-life figure with a warm smile, a deep voice and a transparent style. I was immediately drawn to his right-to-the point, Christ-centered wisdom. Five years later, I'm thankful to call him a friend and am still learning from him. I'm thrilled Simon has written *Jesus Is My CEO* to share some of that wisdom with you, as well! Enjoy!"

–Jeff Thomas
Archetype Wealth Partners Founder/CEO

"It has been my sincere joy to call Simon Lee friend and brother in Christ over the last 15 years. As a fellow Christian business owner, C12 member, ministry partner and long-time client of Simon Lee's office supply company, I have always appreciated Simon's zeal for Jesus, prayer, his family, the church and business as ministry. Simon communicates truth in love to those around him and leads with radical obedience and generosity. My favorite reminder from Simon is, '99% surrender is not surrender'. In these pages, you will be challenged and encouraged with Simon's practical insights that are based on real world experience and many years of walking with the Lord through the ups and downs of life, ministry and business."

–Todd Stewart
Gulf Winds International Inc. Chairman/Owner

"The founder of C12, Buck Jacobs, is famous for saying 'Priorities are what you DO; everything else is just TALK.' We now say 'Do > Talk,' but you get the point. There's a ton of books, theories, voices, researchers and commentators around business. It's a messy art, but at the end of the day, as a follower of Jesus and steward of business—which is really a bunch of people organized to serve people in a way that honors God—it comes down to what you do with the opportunity you have. Let Simon provoke you to think differently about how you would live and lead if you truly embraced Jesus as your CEO in business!"

–Mike Sharrow
C12 Business Forums CEO

CONTENTS

INTRODUCTION

You'VE PROBABLY READ lots of business books in your lifetime, even some of the biggest and best such as *The Effective Executive* by Peter Drucker, *The Innovator's Dilemma* by Clayton Christensen, *Influence* by Robert Cialdini, or *Zero to One* by Peter Theil. We entrepreneurs and business leaders go to business books to find solutions to our challenges, to find ways to grow our businesses, and to grow personally. I've also read many business books during my career as an entrepreneur. While this book you're holding in your hands might not be the best you've ever read, it will point you in a new direction, to a book and to a person you may have never considered to be a business mentor. The book I'm referring to is the Bible, and the person is Jesus.

Too often, Christian entrepreneurs and other business leaders ignore the words and actions of Jesus when it comes to their businesses. They embrace Christ in their personal lives but disregard Him at work. They look at the life of Jesus as something that's relevant only for personal issues, family, church, and in personal growth, but not in business. As a life-long entrepreneur, I've grown to understand the importance of putting Jesus at the center of my company. Just because Jesus doesn't have an MBA doesn't mean he can't be my CEO. This book outlines why and how you, an entrepreneur, can reposition how to believe about Jesus and your business. It's more than just a practical guide—it is an inspiration and motivation for a new kind of business, with Jesus at the center.

I've seen my business grow considerably since I started it eighteen years ago. I've certainly seen ebbs and flows, and I've experienced many challenges, but I can honestly say that in all the years I've been an entrepreneur, I've rarely been tempted to give up. Why? I don't give up because I'm called by God, and Jesus is my CEO.

There's a difference between being a driven entrepreneur and being a called entrepreneur. Highly driven individuals can make great entrepreneurs, be highly successful, and make good decisions. But when the going gets tough (and it always does), only the called persevere. If the foundation of your business is grounded in calling, God's calling, then you don't have to rely on your own strength. Driven individuals are solo operators. They rely on their own strength because they're not called.

In this book, we'll explore what it means to turn your company over, not to another person or a group of people, but to Jesus. Jesus is sovereign, omnipresent, all-powerful, all-knowing, merciful, and full of grace. Have you ever hired anyone who possesses all of those attributes? I don't think so! Turning your company over to Jesus might be the hardest thing you ever did. We entrepreneurs are famous for holding tight control over our businesses. Many of us are micro-managers while others might not be overly controlling, but still, we hold the reins and don't often let go. But I will show you from my own experience that letting go will eventually become the easiest thing you ever did.

Now, take a CEO journey with me. Let's discover how to make Jesus your CEO and learn some valuable leadership and management lessons along the way. Whether you're an emerging start-up or a mature multi-million dollar company, I promise that you'll be inspired and challenged!

1

BE A CHRIST-OWNED CEO

TRIED TO do it all by myself. As the CEO of a fast-growing company, I mustered up all the perseverance and foresight I could humanly find, put on my superhero cape, and went to the office each and every day, determined to succeed in my own strength. I was like a CEO out of a Marvel movie. But guess what happened? I still failed. I was an anxiety-ridden mess, and all my plans lay in ruin.

They say you have to hit rock bottom to find your way back to the top. I suppose you could say that's what happened to me. Gratefully, I discovered there's a better way to be a CEO, the way God intended and showed us in His Word. I found out the hard way that there's a big difference between a CEO who's a believer and the CEO of a Christ-owned business. Once I handed my company over to Jesus, suddenly the stress lifted and my company came back to life. Let me explain.

You see, God owns everything. The Bible says, "For every house is built by someone, but the builder of all things is God" (Hebrews 3:4). The problem for most CEOs is that they are so independent, so focused, and so entrepreneurial that they take on a superhero mentality and try to do it all by themselves. They literally forget that God owns it all. While they build their houses (their businesses), they forget that God is the true builder.

Most CEOs I know are very hard workers. To their credit, they are among the smartest and most determined people I know. But this can become their Achilles' heel. They become too smart for their own good. At first, this mentality works well, despite some bumps in the road. But as a business grows and becomes more complex, the bumps become mountains. The CEO becomes overwhelmed and stressed out. But they try to persevere in their own strength. This is when so many CEOs burn out, make bad decisions, and crash their companies. They become bad bosses, and their personal lives take a real toll. I've known some to come self-destructive and hurt the ones they love.

Once you hand your business over to Christ, place Him at the helm, and appoint Him as the CEO, you'll find a new way that will help both you and your business. Jesus may not have an MBA, but he is the greatest CEO. It's not enough to be a Christian who owns a company. If you're still running it in your own strength and your own "smarts," you'll find yourself in the same predicament as a CEO who's not a believer. But if you can truly make Jesus the CEO, you'll (finally!) find the kind of eternal success and heavenly fulfillment you've been looking for. I'm not saying you won't find trouble or face challenges. But I am saying that with Jesus in charge, the troubles and challenges won't topple you.

Jesus said, "Come to me, all you who are weary and burdened, and I will give you rest. Take my yoke upon you and learn from me, for I am gentle and humble in heart, and you will find rest for your souls. For my yoke is easy and my burden is light" (Matthew 11:28–30). Did you get that? You don't have to take on all the pressures of a CEO. You can let Jesus take that on for you. He wants to give you rest. He wants to alleviate the stress. He wants to lift the burden of cash-flow issues, HR issues, customer service issues, legal issues, regulatory issues, ALL your CEO issues! When Jesus is in charge, you can let the sovereignty of God reign, and there's no better place to be than under God's management.

The other benefit to a Christ-owned business is learning how to discern God's wisdom for your life and organization. The Bible says, "If any of you lacks wisdom, let him ask God, who gives generously to all without reproach, and it will be given him" (James 1:5). Sometimes we make things so much harder than they need to be. As the CEO, you don't have to come up with all the solutions on your own. You simply need to pray and ASK GOD for help. He wants to make your yoke easy and to give you the wisdom you need to make sound decisions. When you go to God in prayer and freely give your organization up to Him, you'll find the answers you've been looking for, not in your own wisdom but by God's grace.

This book will help show you the way toward creating and growing a Christ-owned business. It's not about being "churchy." It's not about packing your staff members into the conference room, playing worship music, and bringing in your pastor to preach to them. It's not about transplanting local church service models into a business setting. I'm a for-profit CEO focused on creating and growing revenue and profit. But I am always looking for ways to keep Christ at the helm. I want to help you do the same. As you read along and journey with me, you'll probably relate to many of the challenges I write about. That's because you and I are a part of a small group of people called CEOs. We have big vision, great goals, and lofty dreams. So let's make Jesus our CEO and grow together. Jesus may not have an MBA, but he is the greatest CEO!

2

BE PRESENT

I'M GOING TO share something with you that will seem obvious, but is also obviously a big problem for many CEOs I know. Many of them are not present. I mean that literally and figuratively. Are you a present CEO? Are you even aware if you are not present? CEOs who "manage" in absentia are more common than you think.

Some CEOs I know are literally and physically not very present in their own organizations. They drop into the office occasionally, tend to a few things, and then bolt. They travel, play golf, and pretend to work but hardly work. These CEOs are eventually blindsided by big problems that they didn't see because they weren't there. Then they blame others, but the end result is that they take the brunt of the ensuing disasters. I'll soon explain.

Other CEOs I know are physically present, but in every other way, they are absent. They hide from their staff, their customers, and even sometimes from spouses and families. They are present but mentally and emotionally absent. Sometimes they are holed up in their offices with the doors closed. Or they show up late and leave early, make it appear as if they are present, but in reality they are hiding. My message to these CEOs: You'd be a better leader if you were present when you showed up.

An absent CEO, either literally or figuratively, is like an absent spouse or parent. It creates a vacuum that will be filled by someone else and eventually lead to chaos. If you aren't around, someone else will step in and steal your spouse, steal your family, steal what you've worked hard for and love. This analogy is not absolute. I am sure there are situations where a trusted senior executive can "fill the shoes" of the CEO, but over the long run, such a working relationship can create great risks to the organization, unbeknownst to the CEO, until it's too late. Don't let this become you!

Jesus is always present. He presents for us the supreme example of leadership in the Gospel of John where he tells us, "I am the good shepherd. The good shepherd lays down his life for the sheep. The hired hand is not the shepherd and does not own the sheep. So when he sees the wolf coming, he abandons the sheep and runs away. Then the wolf attacks the flock and scatters it. The man runs away because he is a hired hand and cares nothing for the sheep" (John 10:11–12). Did you get that? Jesus warns that passing off your presence to a "hired hand" will result in losing your sheep!

You know you're not very present if you don't even show up at your own business. If you don't know your customers, if you hardly know your staff, if you miss things that you only hear about after the fact, then you're clearly not present. You know who you are. But how do you know if you're present but absent? Look for these signs:

- Your ego has taken over. You're "right" most of the time and dismiss everyone else.

- You avoid situations where you might be criticized or conflict may occur.

- You are hooked on technology but not people.

- Everything seems boring to you. You've lost your passion and excitement.

- You're easily angered and lose patience, even with trivial things.

- You hate meeting with your team and you avoid conversations.

- You spend an inordinate amount of time poring over numbers rather than with your staff.

Try to put yourself in your old shoes. Remember when you had a zealous passion for your work? You were ever present with your team and enjoyed their fellowship. You cared for them individually and corporately. Many times we CEOs become absent simply because the business gets complicated. The pressures and stress of running the business tend to make us want to run away from it. I encourage you to press on with Jesus. Remember to place Him at the center, and don't fool yourself into thinking you're in charge. God is in charge! If you lean heavily on Jesus, giving your problems up to Him in prayer, it's easier to be present and to be a "good shepherd" to your sheep.

3

SURRENDER YOUR BUSINESS

A GOOD CEO wears a lot of hats. In fact, the acronym C.E.O. is really a misnomer. A good CEO is a lot more than a chief executive officer. To be effective, he has to get in the trenches and be the "chief" of a lot of things. As a result, sometimes a CEO becomes a micromanager, not necessarily to a fault, but because at times he needs to be.

Over time, however, this can become a problem. Micromanagement can create bottlenecks in an organization, which hampers speed of execution, a key ingredient of scalability. It can also distract a CEO from the most important tasks: thinking about the big picture, drumming up business, and finding resources to make everything run smoothly.

Micromanagement is all about surrendering, and surrendering is a tough thing to do. Even the best CEOs have a hard time doing it. As the CEO of a successful, still growing company for nearly twenty years, I can attest to this fact. It's a daily challenge to let go and just lead. But I want to share with you something else about letting go, something that is even more important than letting go of the daily grind of your business. I want to share with you about surrendering your life, and your entire business, to Jesus.

Most CEOs I know who say they have surrendered their business to God, they've surrendered up to 99 percent of it, at best. But 99 percent surrender is not surrender. Did the Germans surrender 99 percent at the end of World War II? Did the Confederacy surrender 99 percent to the Union at the end of the Civil War? Surrender means surrender. It means total abandonment. You can't partially surrender.

The idea that we as Christian can pick and choose what we can or cannot let go of is not from the Gospel. It's a false narrative that is often ingrained in us by Western culture Christianity. To surrender is often a confusing concept to CEOs because they are so accustomed to managing everything by themselves. They often live by the opposite: control and micromanagement. But if you don't surrender yourself and your business 100 percent, then that's the same as zero percent.

When you asked Jesus to come into your life, and when you asked Him to become the CEO of your company, you made a commitment to let go of everything, not just what you're comfortable surrendering to Him. If you surrender what is comfortable, you'll end up giving God the easy things. You'll hold on tightly to the hard things, the things that you MOST need to give over to Him. It's similar to how you sometimes micromanage your business. If you hold on to it all, you will end up losing it all. The only option is to surrender 100 percent.

Why are you so afraid to give Jesus 100 percent of your business? If you're like me, you sometimes doubt Jesus knows enough to run your business. You think Jesus doesn't have an MBA. Jesus never started a business. Jesus didn't have to meet payroll. Jesus didn't have to recruit, train, and sometimes fire staff. Jesus didn't have to build a website, process credit cards, and manage financials. I once believed all of this. But I discovered the absolute joy and peace that overcame me and my business when I surrendered 100 percent of it to Him.

I want to encourage you to look at your life and your business, and ask yourself: Have I surrendered 100 percent, or am I still holding on? Surrender is not a "one and done" deal. It's a daily habit, just like looking at your bank account every day. Also be mindful that surrender is not the same as compliance. It has nothing to do with your willpower. In fact, it's the opposite of your willpower. It's all about giving Jesus the power, letting go and giving it all to Him, 100 percent.

4

LEARN TO LEAD YOURSELF FIRST

IF YOU'RE A CEO, then you're a leader. It doesn't necessarily make you a great leader, or even a good leader, but like it or not, you're a leader. There are many different types of leaders and leadership styles. You might be a charismatic leader, a servant leader, a more autocratic or bureaucratic leader, or even a laissez-faire leader who is more apt to let others lead the way. Whatever style of leadership you embody, it's important that you begin to understand yourself and how you lead. Leaders don't lead if they don't know who they are or how they lead. Before you can lead others, you need to learn how to lead yourself.

Self-leadership is the first step to becoming an extraordinary leader. Many CEOs I know are more interested in leading others than leading themselves. Yet they flounder because they've not learned the secret to becoming a great leader: self-leadership.

What do I mean? For better or for worse, you bring yourself to every important (or unimportant) encounter you confront. You bring your own personality, your background and experiences, and all of your strengths and weaknesses into each situation. The inward you is outwardly exposed. Whoever you are on the job site, that's the way others perceive you. They may not know or understand it, but in fact they are seeing you from the inside out. So it's vitally important you understand who you are, and even more so that you take control of and lead yourself.

I like Peter Drucker's more simplified explanation: being a self-leader is to serve as chief, captain, or CEO of one's own life. Even if you don't have a leadership title, you are still a self-leader. Self-leadership describes how you lead your own life—setting your course, following it, and correcting it as you go. Life and business are intertwined, so it also reflects how you work with clients, sales prospects, colleagues, and the other leaders in your organization. Self-leadership is something that needs continual focus. One of the best ways to foster innovation and performance is through autonomy and time spent with God.

Let me explain it this way: Leadership is the ability to influence people to get things done. Meanwhile, self-leadership is the ability to consciously influence yourself and to manage your own thoughts, emotions, and actions. I've attended countless leadership conferences and seminars, and in almost all cases, they focus on leading other people. Minimal attention, however, is paid to leading self, the process of observing and managing one's own thoughts, emotions, actions, and behaviors. For a Christian CEO, this also includes your own sinful nature and how you're working it out with God. How can you expect others to follow your lead if they see you're not good at leading yourself?

When I read the Bible, I see how so many great leaders spend time alone with God, from Moses on the mountain to Saul of Tarsus, who spent at least several years in Arabia (including Damascus and the surrounding desert) after his conversion. Even Jesus, after being baptized, spent forty days alone in the desert. I believe they were not only spending time with the Lord better understanding Him. I believe they were also growing in understanding themselves and who they were in the Lord. These were times of great self-discovery.

You've probably learned this already as a leader and CEO, and maybe the hard way: When you fail, you can point at yourself. Blaming other people when things go bad never helps. If you don't learn to take full responsibility, you'll end up in a vicious circle and never experience success. I know CEOs who are constantly blaming other people. Guess what? They do this endlessly until they are so exasperated, they quit! If they'd only own up to themselves, take responsibility, and begin to lead themselves, they'd finally find the success they've been looking for.

Do you lead yourself? Are you taking appropriate actions to manage your own self? Get away with God and ask Him to help prepare you for the road ahead. Here is the good news. You are not alone. He will lead you and guide you. Invite his presence daily to work in and through you.

5

YOU LIVE AND WORK IN TWO KINGDOMS

RUNNING A COMPANY is hard work in a very practical and earthly sense, for both Christian CEOs and for those who do not believe in Jesus. Work is work, yet the "secular work" world is neutral. Here we all do our work and manage all of the necessary activities of running a business. This is true for all business owners, Christian or not. But there is another realm at work, and it's important to be attuned to it. Let me explain.

As Bible-believing Christians, we know that concurrent with our present earthly business operation, but totally different in nature and destiny, is another world where spiritual forces are also hard at work. There are two totally diverse kingdoms, one of our God and another of Satan who captains and administers it by his demons. Until you, as a CEO, recognize the difference between these two kingdoms and allow Jesus to take charge of your company, you will have trouble recognizing when the spiritual forces are at work against you and your company.

Always remember that Satan does not want you to succeed, and his demons are determined to see your company fail. If you've dedicated yourself and your business to God, then you're operating not only in the physical realm but also in spiritual realms.

There are two different kingdoms on earth—namely, the kingdom of this world and the kingdom of Christ. These two kingdoms cannot share nor have communion with each other. Business leaders in the kingdom of this world are born of the flesh and are earthly and carnally minded. Business leaders who operate in the kingdom of Jesus are reborn of the Holy Spirit, are living according to the Spirit, and are spiritually minded. Business leaders in the kingdom of the world are equipped for leading with their carnal weapons only, but leaders in Christ's kingdom are equipped with spiritual weapons—the armor of God, the shield of faith, and the sword of the Spirit to fight against the devil, the world, and their own flesh, together with all that arises against God and His Word.

This is something too many Christian CEOs take too lightly. They forget that even in running their businesses, there is spiritual warfare going on all around. This may sound dramatic, but you are in a daily spiritual battle. There are forces of evil in this world that will not leave any facet of your business unpursued, from your finances to HR to your vendor relationships and customers. As a CEO, you have a responsibility not only to influence the well-being of your organization, but through fervent prayer using the Word of God, you can also cast down organizational strongholds and demonic forces that challenge the integrity, loyalty, and faithfulness of everyone in and around you.

Although Satan is strategic, resourceful, and the ultimate opportunist, our Heavenly Father is so much more. When the attack comes, heed the advice of James: "Submit yourselves, then, to God. Resist the devil, and he will flee from you" (James 4:7 NIV). As a company, we are constantly waging war in a very practical way. In a spiritual way, we:

- Are strong in the Lord and draw our strength from Him (Ephesians 6:10).

- Put on God's armor and resist the strategies of the devil (Ephesians 6:11).

- Dress for battle in God's armor; resist Satan and stand your ground (Ephesians 6:13).

- Base our actions on truth, integrity, and moral correctness (Ephesians 6:14).

- Trust in our salvation and in the power of God's Word (Ephesians 6:17).

- Pray at all times, especially in the Spirit (Ephesians 6:18).

- Keep watch and be alert for the next attack (Ephesians 6:18).

6

VISION AND MISSION

WHEN JESUS SHARED the parable of the wise and foolish builders, he was speaking directly to those of us who build things. So as a CEO who builds a business, I take His words very seriously. But when I speak with other CEOs, particularly startup entrepreneurs, I find that many of them skip the vital step of building a strong foundation. They speed their product or service to market, focused squarely on the "sand" and forgetting to build a solid rock on which to build a business. Unfortunately, these businesses often find initial success, sometimes huge success, but then later crumble when times get a little tougher. Long-term success is sacrificed for short-term gain.

How does a CEO, a startup entrepreneur, or any other business leader begin to build a strong foundation? Spend time thinking through, praying about, and writing down the reasons you own your company. Don't let being pragmatic get in the way of this important stage of building a strong foundation of consensus for your organization. If you don't take the time to articulate your vision, your mission, and your core values, you will pay for it later when you're trying to take your company to the next level. It will impact everything including your hiring decisions, where and how to invest your profits, how to compete, and of course, how to define your place in the market. It will also impact your relationship with God and His role in your life and in the life of your company.

Before you can develop a strategic plan, you must know where you're trying to go and be in the future (your vision), why you're doing what you do every day (your mission), and who you are as a company (your core values). These elements form the glue that holds an organization together. You preserve them while your strategies and goals change and flex with the market. You may modify your mission, vision, or values over time, but the intent stays unchanged, so you will have complete clarity when making critical business decisions that impact your future.

Some CEOs stumble when trying to articulate the foundation for their businesses, but I maintain the best vision, mission, and core value statements are simply stated, easy to remember, and not full of fluff with meaningless jargon. So many leaders I talk to can't even remember their vision, mission, and core values! It's also critically important that you are the one who develops and articulates a company's founding principles, with God's help. Don't delegate this very important process to those who don't understand who you are as a leader. This is about YOU and who God has called YOU to be.

Here's what I recommend in plain language. Ask yourself these questions, wherein lies the answers to your vision, mission, and core values. This simple process will help you think about how you want to articulate your company's foundation.

Vision Questions:

- Who do you want to become in the future?

- What do you want to be in the future?

- Where do you see yourself in the future?

Mission Questions:

- Why do you wake up in the morning to do what you do?

- What daily processes and routines do you try to achieve each day?

- What drives you to start and run your company?

Core Values Questions:

- Who are you as a person and as a company?

- What principles are most important to you and to your company?

- What values do you align yourself with as a leader of your company?

Strive to answer these questions with the simplest language you can think of, not lofty or complex language. Use words even a child might understand. Yes it's THAT easy to begin the process of laying the foundation for your business. When I founded my company more than eightteen years ago, I took prayerful time to lay my foundation. Although my vision, mission, and core values have changed some over the years, I can honestly say they haven't changed that much. It provided a strong foundation for a business that has grown and become stable, even when enduring difficult times. Maybe this will also help you as you develop your company's foundation.

Our Vision

To donate millions of dollars to our non-profit partners by becoming one of the largest independent retailers in the U.S.

Our Mission

To advance God's kingdom by donating 50 percent of corporate profits to change lives while providing world-class service to our customers.

Our Core Values

1. **Excellence**

   We will give our best in everything that we do and provide quality products to all of our customers. We will treat each other with the dignity and respect that each person deserves.

2. **Integrity**

   We will maintain the highest ethical standards in all of our interactions as a company and as individuals.

3. **Selflessness**

   We will always put customers first. Serving our customers will always be our #1 priority.

7

WHAT TO DO ABOUT ANXIETY

B EING AN ENTREPRENEUR and CEO comes with the immense responsibility of continually driving your company's vision, purpose, and
operations. There are daily HR issues, cash flow issues, legal issues, and
an abundance of related items to worry about. People depend on you,
and any wrong move might impact everyone who works for you. The
anxiety and depression that result from all this pressure are real. Hiding
your anxiety without taking steps to overcome it only makes things worse.

Thankfully, we serve a BIG God who can take the anxiety away, but
not in a way that you might expect. Let me explain.

When our company was in its infancy, I would lie awake at night
worrying. I worried about everything and imagined all sorts of potential threats. I went from Chief Executive Officer to Chief Worry Officer,
particularly during our downturns, crises, and setbacks. Some CEOs
I know find their anxiety is so severe and so constant that it drastically
affects their day-to-day living.

It can become a vicious circle where being anxious creates more
anxiety, as if fighting fire with fire. It was not this way for me, but even
still, the anxiety was not easy to bear.

There are many practical steps you can take to reduce your anxiety, such as taking walks, learning relaxation techniques, limiting caffeine intake, getting sleep and rest, and exercising. But prayer is the most important, and as a believer, this is what I did. I got on my knees and asked God to take away my anxiety. I begged God to lift all worry off my shoulders and place it on the cross. I know that God did help me during this time, but I also realize now that I was praying for the wrong thing.

"Praying for the wrong thing?" you ask. Yes, you read that correctly. I was praying for God to take away my anxiety, to give me peace, but not to take over. I was not asking God to be King and Lord of my company. I was just asking God to make me a better and calmer leader. I was praying so I would FEEL better when I should have been praying for God to be MY GOD and for Jesus to be my CEO. It was the wrong prayer.

Philippians 4:7 says, "Be anxious for nothing, but in everything, by prayer and petition, with thanksgiving, present your requests to God. And the peace of God, which surpasses all understanding, will guard your hearts and your minds in Christ Jesus." We agree, of course, with this scripture. But have you wondered WHY and HOW the peace of God surpasses all understanding? The Bible doesn't instruct us to pray for God to magically remove our anxieties. It asks us to present them to God and then to let God take over. It's not about removing your anxieties. It's about removing yourself from the throne and placing God on it. I like what A.W. Tozer once wrote, "As God is exalted to the right place in our lives, a thousand problems are solved all at once."

After eighteen years, I learned better how to pray about my anxieties, which of course I still have today. All business owners have anxieties. But I've learned better how to place God first, God second, and God third, until all that's left is God. When Jesus is your CEO, your anxieties are lifted because He is in control, not you. The reason we worry is because we try to be in control. Do you think God will lift all worry off of you when you pray but then push God out? Do you think God is interested in your health and well-being when after you pray, you leave God on the shelf and go back to your company as the CEO? God loves you, and He wants to work through you and your company, but if you demand that He heal you while letting you run things, then I fear you will still have to deal with your anxieties.

If you need the words to pray, join me with these words:

Jesus, You are the King and Lord of my life and my company. You are the CEO. I give up all control to You, for You are sovereign in all things. I relinquish my authority, my reign, and my dominance over every part of my life and company. Take over, Lord, and run my company. Amen!

8

FOCUS ON TRUE SUCCESS

For four years, I had worked long and hard at growing my company. It was a thrilling yet exhausting adventure, and we finally had made a profit. It wasn't much, just $10,000, but we were out now of the red and into the black. It was a milestone to be sure, and I decided to give 50 percent of it away to charity (something I still do today). After attending the charity event, I expected to feel joyful and fulfilled, but on the contrary, I felt dejected. I should have been leaping for joy, not only because I earned a profit, but also because I was able to help others who needed the money more than I did. But no, my emotions lay flat, and I had to go to the Lord about it. You see, after working so hard for so many years, I didn't feel like a successful CEO. It wasn't enough money. After so much work, there wasn't much left over.

So I went to God and asked Him to hear me out. I talked to Him about my hard work, my business, how I overcame so many challenges, and my top-line revenue and bottom-line profit. Sometimes when you pray, you have to wait patiently for God to answer you, but during this particular time, God spoke to me instantly and clearly. He didn't shame me or put me down. He didn't offer condolences or exhortations. He told me something I will never forget: My business, His business, was not to be measured by my profit-and-loss statement and my balance sheet. He said to me, "Simon, I don't measure or monitor your success based on your financial statements. I just want you to be faithful. I care more about your heart than your numbers."

It was an emotional time for me, and afterwards I felt a complete sense of joy and release. I realized that God loved me no matter how the company performed according to the world's standards. He wasn't looking for an ace CEO, but just someone who was a faithful CEO according to His Word. This was a turning point for me, in terms of how I led my company as a CEO and how I lived my life. God was looking for faithfulness, not performance.

In John 15:5–6, Jesus shares with us a parable that is most relevant to CEOs, entrepreneurs, and business leaders. I want you to meditate on this and let it sink into your heart, because you probably sometimes feel the way I did. Jesus said, "I am the vine; you are the branches. If a man remains in me and I in him, he will bear much fruit; apart from me you can do nothing. If anyone does not remain in me, he is like a branch that is thrown away and withers; such branches are picked up, thrown into the fire and burned." Did you get that? Jesus is the vine, not your company. You are the branch, not your company. It's about you and God, and you and God only. Don't fool yourself into thinking anything else.

Jesus is your sole source of true security, true wealth, and true profitability. Remain faithful to Him, allow yourself to be pruned when necessary, and you will produce much fruit. The bearing of fruit depends on dependence on Him, not your financial statements. It depends on your connection to God and how to seek Him. As soon as you think you can produce anything based on your own sovereignty, your own efforts, or your own sense of independence, you'll feel lost and dejected as a CEO.

While it's important to measure and monitor all aspects of your business, including your financial statements, that's not where you should look for confidence. God is saying, "Job well done" when you're faithful to Him in prayer and action, not when your CPA says your business is doing well. Since my prayer time many years ago, my company has grown, but not without many challenges, of course. But never again did I feel a sense of shame or dejection. I understood that true success is earned by being faithful to Him, not by any other measure.

"Give, and it shall be given unto you; good measure, pressed down, and shaken together, and running over, shall men give into your bosom. For with the same measure that ye mete withal it shall be measured to you again" (Luke 6:38–39).

9

HEARING THE VOICE OF GOD

W E ALL WANT to hear from God, right? Every Christian CEO I know desperately wants to hear the voice of God for his business. I've never met one who didn't want to hear God's voice. And I'm quite sure that you, the reader of this book, is praying for God to share with you His ideas, His plans, and His direction for you and your business. You want Him to speak now and loudly!

But I'm quite sure that you struggle to hear His voice. You believe He wants to speak to you, but you can't always hear what He is saying. The question is not DO you want to hear from the Lord. Of course you do. The question is HOW you hear from the Lord to make decisions.

We know that God is always speaking. The problem isn't that God is not speaking. The problem is we're not hearing Him speak. As we're challenged sometimes to hear and listen to the voice of God to make important decisions, I find that people tend to fall into five failed categories, usually out of impatience. The results are flippant decisions, often later regretted.

Do these people sound familiar to you?

I already have a plan, God,
so bless me with A, B, or C!

These individuals have already made up their minds, all by themselves. They're ready to run, and they just want God to bless them with their decision. Bless me, God! Send it now because I'm ready to move. I'm a good Christian, so just give me one of my options.

I love doors, God, so walk with
me every time a door opens!

I hear this a lot. You find an open door to a new opportunity, so you just walk in unannounced. Every time a door opens, you just jump through it and say, "Let's go, God!" In fact, you find so many open doors, you spend most of your time walking from door to door, asking God to be your wingman.

I love the freedom you give me, God,
to make my own decisions!

God is sovereign and He loves me, so I'm going to move on with my freedom in Christ. I'll make my decisions, and if I'm wrong, then God will take care of my mistakes. I'm free in Christ, and I'm not going to worry about making the wrong decision. God is good all the time!

The Bible will be my only guide, God,
so speak to me through your Word!

This person rightly spends time in the Word. He scours scripture for answers, but gets confused and befuddled when he can't find answers to specific questions. Yes, scripture has all the answers to life, but when it comes to specific advice, there are various ways in which scripture reminds us to lean on.

I can't wait, God, so therefore I'm going to do it now!

This person puts a timer on God, and when God doesn't provide a quick answer, he moves forward. He is in a hurry and assumes if he doesn't hear from God loudly and clearly, that means God must be saying "yes."

I think we can all admit that we've been one of the above people at least once in our lives. Maybe you're stuck as one of these people today. When I started as an entrepreneur and CEO, I surely struggled to hear God's voice. I wanted Him to speak, but I felt that He was silent, and when making important decisions, I was stumped! But then the Lord shared with me that my impatience was rooted in my disobedience.

Here's what Paul said: "Since we live by the Spirit, let us keep step with the Spirit" (Galatians 5:25). The problem was that I was always trying to be one step ahead of the Lord. Instead of trying to keep in step with the Spirit, I was trying to be the pacemaker. I was leading, not God. I was leading and looking back at God, instead of letting Him be my CEO. When I finally resolved to let Jesus be the CEO, I was able to hear His voice. We CEOs are type-A, driven, high-strung, high-powered people. We forget that we cannot run our companies in our own strength. When we do, we don't hear any other voice than our own. Learn to be in step with the Spirit. When you do, God will speak into your life!

Most people when they first discover that God can actually speak to them, the number one obstacle they will go through is whether it is their own voice or God's voice. Allow me to use an analogy of riding a bicycle. When we first start riding a bicycle, there will be plenty of falls. Hearing the voice of God in the beginning will feel very similar. We simply don't know if it is our voice or God's voice. The first and foremost thing we must do when we journey into this space is to spend regular time in His word and prayer. Our intimacy with God is primary. If you don't have a regular devotional time with our Lord first, please do this first above all. You will not be able to discern well if you don't have an intimate relationship with our Savior.

As you are discerning and you are not sure whether it is your voice and God's voice, I would simply walk into it by faith. For example, you are at a restaurant and you sensed that you need to share the gospel with the waitress. You are not sure if that is your own will or if it is God's will. But you simply share with her anyways not knowing 100% if it was God's voice or not. God is very pleased when we walk by faith. He will not condemn you or tell you that you are wrong. That is not the heart of our Father. Our Father simply wants us to pursue Him and have an intimate relationship with him where we are following His will in our lives.

This is the process of learning to hear from God. Walk slowly first and simply walk into it by faith. If you are wrong, it is ok. God forgives you. Simply trust Him again next time. The more you walk by faith the more you will know His voice.

The second thing that I like caution is to make sure we never use "God told me this or God told you this". We try to avoid "Thus said the Lord" at all cost. We are sinners in need of God's grace. We are not perfect people. We will make mistake time to time hearing from God and that is ok. The way we can to present ourselves in regard to God's voice is with humility and caution. The way we can way to say is "I sensed God is tell me to do this. Would you pray with me and help me discern if this is indeed God's will." The word sense is key here. We are not saying we are 100% correct. We are sensing God's voice and we could be wrong. We always want to pray when we think we heard from God and when possible, we want to discern and pray with others. To walk in humility and know that we make mistakes is absolutely paramount to hearing God's voice.

I know that once we believe this and walk in this that God will use us powerfully to expand the company that God has given us. His power and love will lead us to lead others better and by hearing God's voice, we will experience Him in such an intimate way that you will fall more in love with our Savior.

10

BE SATISFIED

IF YOU THINK that starting and running your own company will bring you a sense of contentment, I want you to think again. If you think that being your own boss will end your days of inner turmoil and frustration, I want you to think again. If you think that being a CEO will finally help you feel as if you've achieved something significant in life, I want you to think again.

This will come as a hard word to some readers, but you won't find the satisfaction you're looking for simply by being an entrepreneur or business owner. In fact—and I say this from experience—it will make you feel even less satisfied and content. Instead of feeling a sense of freedom, you'll pile feelings of anxiety on top of discontentment! But I can also say from experience that you can (and will) find the contentment you're looking for—just not in your business.

Some Christian CEOs I counsel recite to me Philippians 4:13, "I can do all this through him who gives me strength," as they muscle through their business challenges. Yet they are muscling through on the wrong premise. They are aiming for the wrong goal. They are looking for more personal satisfaction. They feel that they can simply keep running harder for the finish line, and with God's help, they'll find the strength to keep going and finally be content. My advice is to look at what Paul says in the few verses *before* Philippians 4:13. Context is so important when reading the Bible. Look at what Paul is saying:

I rejoiced greatly in the Lord that at last you renewed your concern for me. Indeed, you were concerned, but you had no opportunity to show it. I am not saying this because I am in need, for I have learned to be content whatever the circumstances. I know what it is to be in need, and I know what it is to have plenty. I have learned the secret of being content in any and every situation, whether well fed or hungry, whether living in plenty or in want. I can do all this through him who gives me strength. (Philippians 4:10–13)

Did you get that? Paul shares that he has "learned to be content whatever the circumstances" before he says he "can do all things." He tells us that he's learned a secret that has transformed his life and work. The secret is learning to be joyful and satisfied in the Lord and His goodness, rather than in work.

The Apostle Paul, who wrote thirteen of the twenty-seven books in the New Testament, was also an entrepreneur, just like you. He was an entrepreneur who made tents for a living. Like other Jewish men, Paul had been taught this trade as a boy, and he was also taught how to make money with it. Even after his salvation and during his missionary work, Paul was still a business entrepreneur. "You yourselves know that these hands ministered to my own needs and to the men who were with me. In everything I showed you that by working hard in this manner you must help the weak and remember the words of the Lord Jesus, that He Himself said, 'It is more blessed to give than to receive'" (Acts 20:33–35).

Was it Paul's business acumen and success that brought him satisfaction? Did making tents help Paul to feel content? Paul probably did quite well as a tent-making entrepreneur. But what was it that *finally* made Paul feel satisfied? He learned the secret, and it was not in his business activities but in his relationship with the Lord Jesus. After meeting Jesus, Paul no longer yearned for more material wealth, more power, more control, or a bigger and more profitable business. Jesus fulfilled all his needs and gave him a secret strength so he could "do all things." He could do all things because he no longer felt dissatisfaction. Paul's incredible strength, perseverance, and happiness were not the result of a better business, but of a better relationship with the Lord.

The joy of the Lord, my friend, will give you strength so you can press on in His good will for you and your business. Make Jesus your CEO, and you'll not worry about finding contentment. You'll be content and strong for the journey!

11

PRAY WHILE YOU PLAN

TRADITIONALLY, CHURCHES, MINISTRIES, and Christian non-profit organizations are strong on prayer but weak on execution. Business organizations, including Christian business organizations, are often strong on execution but weak on prayer. And they tend to view prayer and planning as mutually exclusive. They do them separately. They pray about something, but not during planning. Or they plan something but not during prayer.

As a CEO who has learned to put Jesus in charge of my company, I've learned to lean on Proverbs 16:9: "In their hearts humans plan their course, but the Lord establishes their steps." This is one of the most important scriptures, in my view, because it's where God tells us that prayer and planning should be simultaneous activities. He wants us to integrate prayer and planning into everything we do, together and at the same time. Does this surprise you?

I've observed that some Christian business leaders are afraid to integrate prayer into their business planning because they don't think God cares as much about business as He does about ministry. On the contrary, if you're leading a Christian business, God is using you as a minister of the Gospel. There is no difference between you and a vocational minister! God is using you according to His will and purpose. Yes, sometimes Christian business leaders will pray when they are in trouble, stressed out, or otherwise need God's help. But they don't consistently include prayer as a part of their business planning process.

I encourage you to do what we do: *We pray as we plan, and we plan as we pray.* We never stop doing either as we work our way through each business day. Every time we meet to discuss business decisions, we pray. It's an actual part of our business process. Planning and praying are simultaneous.

There are so many reasons to pray as you plan. We pray to communicate with God, because communication with God is an absolutely essential part of knowing what He wants us to do as a business. We pray because He invited us to ask Him for whatever we want, just as He invited Solomon to ask for whatever he wanted. That kind of divine generosity and open-heartedness will call us to ask thoughtfully, like Solomon, with an awareness of how big, powerful, and loving God is. We pray because we can do nothing without God and we need Him desperately. We pray because it reminds us that our business is completely dependent on God.

God is not asking you to be an expert business planner. He doesn't expect you to be the perfect business planner. God is simply asking you to be faithful in Him. When you submit to Him and relinquish all control, you don't have to worry about the end result. You are in charge of one thing, and that's your faithfulness. So think about yourself as the CEO of faithfulness. Keep praying as you plan, and God will help you plan. He will provide the answers you so desperately seek.

If you're anything like me, you love to plan. You get a sense of satisfaction when Monday rolls around and you know your week is organized and scheduled. But guess what? Even with all the planning in the world, some things never go as expected. Call it what you want, but the James has an explanation: "Whereas you do not know what will happen tomorrow. For what is your life? It is even a vapor that appears for a little time and then vanishes away. Instead you ought to say, 'If the Lord wills, we shall live and do this or that'" (James 4:14–15). He says quite bluntly that we don't know what will happen tomorrow. So if that's the case, you may wonder, should I stop planning? No! Planning is not the problem. James is simply saying we must plan with prayer—asking for wisdom from the Holy Spirit to help us embrace God's timing to know and do His will. Ultimately, we recognize that Jesus knows best.

12

TELL A COMPELLING STORY

MANY ENTREPRENEURS I KNOW seem to think that to launch a successful startup, they have to sell a unique product or service. They try so hard to create something brand new. They fashion themselves more as inventors than as entrepreneurs. Then when we converse about what I do—I sell office supplies—they are incredulous. "How did you start and build such a successful company that sells office supplies?" they ask me. "There are hundreds, maybe even thousands of companies that sell office supplies!" When I show them our growth chart, they are even more astounded at how successful we are at selling something so ordinary.

What do I tell them? First, of course, we run a good company. We work hard, we respect our team members, we work collaboratively to grow our company together, we are careful strategic planners, we're creative marketers, and we serve Jesus. But we also do something most companies don't do: **We have a unique story and we tell it well, everywhere we go.**

What we sell is not unique. But our story is most unique, and that's what attracts customers. In a world where people have a lot of choices, the story may be the deciding factor.

Does your company or organization have a story? Who are you? Where did you come from?

Why are you doing this? I believe the WHY of it is the most important question to answer.

Let me tell you about our WHY. It's why we give to life-changing causes using dollars you're spending every day in an unglamorous category.

In 1996, I went to East Asia on my very first mission trip. While there, I played a short pick-up basketball game with a student from the local university. He slid all over the court in a pair of old dress shoes while I played in Air Jordan athletic shoes. Later, when I asked why he wore dress shoes to play basketball, he quietly replied that they were the only pair of shoes he owned. That one brief encounter transformed my world!

God continued to use mission trips to chisel away at my own desires, and slowly but surely, He replaced them with His desire that I become a servant, a giver of wealth, and a lover of the least of these. I returned from another life-changing mission trip and found myself lying in bed, unable to sleep. When I did sleep, I would dream of the number 50 in neon lights. Then I began to wake up whenever the number 50 appeared! It soon became clear after prayer and consultation with mentors, pastors, and friends that God was calling me to start a company that would donate 50 percent of its profits to change lives. One day, my father came to my office with a check for $50,000 to help start **Buy on Purpose**. My parents supported this mission and gave up their own dream of having their only son taking over their company. Since 2004, Buy on Purpose has supported nonprofit organizations in the Houston area. We are so grateful to run a company, not just for profit, but also to see lives changed. In fact, since then, we've donated more than $500,000 to charitable causes across Houston.

When our customers make a purchase, they know they are helping us fulfill God's call, to be a company that is giving to transform lives. It gives deep meaning to a purchase of something common. This is largely what has caused our company to grow and be successful.

Honestly, I'm hard-pressed to think of a company that doesn't have an interesting foundational story. But I find so many that haven't been well-crafted and told as a part of their mission. Your story is so important. People want to be part of something bigger than themselves. A nameless, faceless business with no real purpose, no story, is not motivating to staff or customers.

Remember what Jesus said when He was walking the shores of the Sea of Galilee? "Come follow me and be fishers of men"! He didn't recruit His disciples with a boring pitch of what it means to be a disciple. He used an everyday common thing, fishing, to create a story. Then as He traveled from village to village, He told more stories. It's why crowds of people gathered to listen. Jesus was the Master Storyteller. Ask Him to help you tell your story!

13

TRUST YOUR TEAM

As a CEO, have you ever thought about how much trust Jesus placed in His disciples? He trusted them implicitly and gave them freedom to be His disciples and to spread the good news after His resurrection and ascension. Jesus spent only three years with His "executive team" before commissioning them to make disciples of all nations. He invested Himself in them, spending time with them, mentoring and teaching, and then He placed the Kingdom of God into their hands. He trusted them, and they trusted Him. I like to use this example when talking about building trust in your executive team.

If you don't build a strong management team, your company will never scale the way you'd like. When you launch a company and it's still in its infancy, you can be the single voice, the sole executor and manager of the company. But as it grows, it's abundantly important that you do not remain the company's only voice. You have to find others and begin to trust them as much as you trust in yourself. For too many entrepreneurs, ego is the biggest obstacle that keeps them from reaching their full potential. They're often reluctant to seek help from people who are more talented and knowledgeable.

I've learned that you need to drop your insecurities and hire the best talent you can afford. Insecurity often discourages entrepreneurs from hiring team members who are smarter than they are. Early in my career, I was hesitant to hire people who were smarter than I was. I didn't want to accept that I might not be the smartest person in the room. I feared losing respect; I thought that, as the leader, I should have all the answers. You may even feel self-conscious that your subordinates might turn to the new team member for guidance instead of you. And while this is a valid concern, it shouldn't keep you from choosing the best candidate—even if that means that you'll no longer be the smartest person on the team. You need other people surrounding you, people who are literally brighter and smarter than you.

To get to that point, you must be able to trust your executive team, and your entire staff, for that matter. Trust is a two-way street. You don't trust until you've been trusted. Give and take must be on both sides, a mutual exchange. So it won't happen immediately, especially if you're a faster growing company with many new team members. Here's what I found is most important when building trust between yourself and your executive team: respect.

Trust starts with respect. Show your staff members that you respect them first, understand what they care about, and trust them in a safe environment. Help them not to fail, but if they do, show them that you are trustworthy by supporting them. That will motivate them more than just throwing out some platitudes about trust as the opposite of micro-managing; trust, but verify. Start with smaller projects, and then as trust builds, you can delegate more and manage less.

Talk a lot, especially at the beginning of the relationship. People may have different value systems for trust, and leading in such an environment requires clear communication. You have to understand what makes a person "tick" before you can honestly and effectively communicate with him. So seek to lead and inspire, but also seek to understand every team member, even on a personal level. We all like to work closely with people who we like. So be likable! Chances are your team will in turn be likable and trustable. I believe it's even important to flat out ask your team, "How am I doing?" Don't be afraid to put yourself out there and ask for constructive criticism. You aren't the perfect boss, right? So find out from those who know you best, your team. They'll trust you more if you're honest with them and seek to become a better leader in their eyes.

These are the things Jesus did. We have no better example of a leader who invested Himself in other people, to build them up and create a movement that spanned the entire earth. I'm glad that Jesus trusted His team so that we can trust Him!

14

DON'T BE AFRAID TO PIVOT

IT'S EASY TO become married to your company's original idea—the original concept, product, or service that you launched and eventually became successful. After all, you spent so much time, energy, and effort to get it off the ground. You're proud of what you accomplished. Why change anything? But what happens when all of your hard work stops paying off? What happens when circumstances that are totally out of your control gradually, or even suddenly, interrupt your business model? It happens to almost every CEO. At some point, your plans change.

This is exactly what happened during the winter of 2020. When the COVID-19 pandemic spread around the world, it took every CEO off guard. Suddenly what had been working for almost all businesses stopped working. Customer bases dried up, supply chains broke down, and people got sick and even died. The pandemic was (and is) a most appropriate example for how not to be married to your original business plan. Things change!

This is why it's important to learn to pivot, and pivot well. What does this mean?

We all make changes to our businesses monthly, weekly, or even daily. But a pivot means to fundamentally change the direction of your business model when you realize it's no longer meeting the needs of the market, which may occur gradually or suddenly. Pivoting is complicated in the context of both startups and mature businesses, and it can have far-reaching consequences. Pivoting is when you make a modification or adjustment in your startup belief or practice. To put it simply, it refers to a shift of direction. So shift carefully, but also know that sometimes it's absolutely necessary. Don't be so attached to your original idea that you fail to pivot and go down with your ship.

The main goal of a pivot is to help a company improve revenue and profits, or even just to survive. Pivoting is not, however, a last-ditch effort to save a company. While pivoting a business can breathe new life into an otherwise struggling business, if you wait too long to pivot, your company may not survive. Also be mindful that when you pivot, you may need to start from scratch and abandon some (or all) of the investments, ideas, and plans that you had previously put into your company. Sometimes it even means overhauling your team. That's why it's important to pivot with prudence and good information. Otherwise a pivot can destroy your company.

If you have been thinking about pivoting your business, then you should know what it entails before you go forward with the move. When COVID-19 came on the scene, our business was hit hard. Since we are in the office supply business, and the nature of the office and supplies changed so abruptly, it didn't take long for us to realize we had to pivot. Suddenly most of our business customers weren't even coming back to the office. This meant their needs changed significantly, in terms of the kinds and amount of products they now needed. If we didn't pivot, I know that our business would have gone under.

How did we successfully pivot? First, we collaboratively as a team put our heads together to find ways to pivot. As the company's CEO, I had to admit that I would not be the one who had all the answers. I relied heavily on my team members who were on the front lines with our customers. So we deployed our team to reach out and talk to our customers. We sought to discover, as soon as possible, what and how their needs changed. I like to think that our discovery was so rapid that we beat many of our competitors to the punch. We were not afraid to pivot. We were not afraid, as a team, to literally throw away some of the work we were most proud of. We re-launched with new products and services that increased our sales by 177 percent the year COVID-19 began and then 255 percent the year after!

My advice to those CEOs who feel that it might be time to pivot is that if you're thinking that way, you may already be too late. So pivot soon. And don't pivot alone but with your team. Once when Jesus was ministering to thousands of people, His disciples begged Jesus to let everyone leave. They were getting hungry, and there was not enough food. What did Jesus do? He pivoted with His team. He asked His disciples to distribute the food they had, and then He worked a miracle. I believe that you and your company can also work a miracle!

15

DEALING WITH PERSECUTION

I F THERE ARE any remaining doubts, the news over the past few years puts it to rest: Christian businesses are increasingly being targeted for their values and beliefs. Our business has also been targeted, and I want to share with you, as a CEO, how we are approaching this fast-growing problem of persecution.

Of course the persecution we are facing is not the same kind that the early church faced. We are not literally being thrown into the lion's den. But wedding venues are forced to cease hosting weddings. Other companies are compelled to jettison whole segments of business. Some small business owners risk losing not only their company but also their life savings in an attempt to defend themselves. This hostility toward biblical truth is forcing Christian CEOs to take a stand, much as the Israelites had to decide in response to Joshua's challenge: "Choose this day whom you will serve. ... But as for me and my house, we will serve the Lord" (Joshua 24:14–15).

What should Christian business owners do about this?

First, you should expect persecution. At the most basic level, we are seeing a collision of worldviews. People will either live according to what God says is true or according to what man says is true. The Bible warns that "all who desire to live godly in Christ Jesus will be persecuted" (2 Timothy 3:12). So when Christian CEOs suffer for taking a biblical stand, they are simply experiencing the expected backlash from a godless culture. Although it may seem that this persecution has materialized recently in America, it is the result of many legal strands being woven together over more than a century, and actually all the way back to the early church. Darkness and light don't go together well; darkness will always want to put out the light. So don't be surprised. The world is doing what the world does.

Second, don't be afraid to be bold. This is not a time to be timid or to hide from the Gospel or compromise your values just for a healthier bottom line. It's also not a time to be stupid. We always say, "Being stupid for Jesus is still being stupid." So while it's important to be aggressive in defending our beliefs, it's also important to find good counsel and to approach the persecution with wisdom.

Let me explain with a real-life example. Our company once won a large, multi-million-dollar contract. Afterwards, the purchaser asked us to remove a signature from our emails, "Sincerely, In Christ." They stated that the signature was offensive to those who don't believe in Christ. In this situation, I didn't launch an expensive lawsuit or publicly challenge the organization, but rather I privately challenged them. I didn't back down, but I used biblical wisdom when I communicated with them about their request. In a telephone conversation, I asked them, "Has anyone ever actually responded negatively to such an email signature?" and "Does our email signature imply, in any way, that we are forcing our beliefs on anyone?" Their answer was no. They conceded and allowed us to use the signature. In this case, my very polite but direct approach worked. All praise to God!

Third, be ready in some cases to launch a legal defense. Unfortunately, there may be cases in which a legal defense becomes necessary. Don't go it alone! Reach out to a reputable organization, such as the Alliance Defending Freedom, the world's largest legal organization committed to protecting religious freedom, free speech, marriage and family, parental rights, and the sanctity of life. A solid legal team can (and does) win cases that protect CEOs and Christian-owned businesses from hostile attacks.

It's important for you to find and fellowship with other Christian CEOs during this time to better learn and understand the issues that are at hand. Persecution is better approached as a unified group of believers, rather than as a lone individual. I'm a big proponent of CEO accountability groups, and I believe during this era in our country's history, it's ever more important. C12 Business Forum is one that I am part of. Check them out!

16

BEWARE OF THE LOVE OF MONEY

A RESEARCHER ONCE asked people who earned $50,000 a year how much *more* they needed to be at peace and feel satisfied. They answered, "$100,000." The researcher then found people who earned $100,000 a year and asked how much *more* money they needed to be at peace and feel satisfied. They answered, "A quarter million dollars a year." Then the researcher found some people who were earning a quarter million dollars a year and asked them how much *more* they needed to be at peace and feel satisfied. They said, "I need to be a millionaire to be fully content." Finally, the researcher found some millionaires and asked them the very same question. The millionaires all said they need one billion dollars to finally be at peace.

It will never be enough, will it? How about you? How much more money do you need to feel good about yourself and your life? Has the love of money entrapped you?

Most sins have a direct or indirect connection to the love of, or craving for, more money. The challenge for entrepreneurs and CEOs is that much of our lives revolve around making money. If we're not careful, we will obsess about it and eventually fall into the trap of craving more and more money until it enslaves us. The great writer and poet Robert Herrick once said, "Who covets more is evermore a slave." The Bible clearly tells us, "For the love of money is the root of all evil: which while some coveted after, they have erred from the faith, and pierced themselves through with many sorrows" (1 Timothy 6:10).

Here's the thing to remind yourself: No matter how much money you crave, you will never be satisfied. You will want more and more and more, but ultimately you will be disappointed and empty. The great CEO and entrepreneur Ted Turner once said, "You can't really spend large amounts of money intelligently on buying things." It's true. The excessive spending of money becomes something only fools do well. Lavishness is never something that people respect or yearn for. If you spend more time thinking about ways to save OR spend your money, then you're in danger of loving money more than anything else, including your family and God. And don't fool yourself into thinking that your family needs your money more than they need you!

One of your priorities as a CEO should be to protect yourself from the love of money, and there are actionable steps you can take to avoid the trap of the greed of living a lavish lifestyle. I encourage you to find at least one accountability partner to help you along the way. You need at least one person in your life to help you avoid the love of money. It's by far the easiest trap to fall into, so don't try to do this by yourself.

There are some actionable steps I've taken since I became an entrepreneur and CEO.

First, ask yourself regularly: Why are you an entrepreneur? Why are you running your business? What drives you? I know that you didn't start your business simply to make money. You could make money working for someone else. You started your business because you have a drive and a passion for the product or service you create and sell. It wasn't about the money in the first place, so don't let it be the last place. Remind yourself regularly why you do what you do, then act like it.

Second, be careful how much you pay yourself and how much profit you take from your company. Many CEOs I know raid their company's bank account in foolish ways. They take more out than they need to, which has negative consequences for their own businesses. You need to invest in your people and your product before you foolishly invest in your own material wealth. I am very conservative in how much I invest in my own material wealth. I pay myself a modest amount to save myself from the love of money.

Finally, try to spend more time looking out for how you foolishly waste money than how you want to treat yourself in lavish ways. Be budget conscious. Find ways to improve your top and bottom line by sticking to a budget, a budget that is shared by you and your team. If you find yourself not paying attention to your company's budget and instead spending money on yourself, then you've fallen into the trap of loving money. Ask your CPA, CFO, or others who are responsible for your money to help you stick to a budget. Ask them you help you be accountable.

Why are you running your company? It's never about the money. It's about the call of God on your life to bring joy, happiness, and Gospel impact to your people and your customers. Stay focused on your calling, not on your money, and you'll find the contentment you've been looking for.

17

BELIEVE IN MIRACLES

GOD IS A GOD of miracles! If there's anything the Bible is clear on, it's that God uses miracles to bless His people and to display His power, with no help from others. God's miraculous power inspires wonder, and it acts as a sign that God is at work in the world. The Bible says, "You are the God who performs miracles; you display your power among the peoples" (Psalm 77:14).

Most believers I know say they believe in miracles. Most of the churches I know say they believe in miracles. Most of the pastors I know say they believe in miracles. Most of the Christian CEOs I know also say they believe in miracles. Yet most of these same CEOs tend to compartmentalize their belief in a miracle-working God. They believe God can work miracles in their own personal lives, in their families, and in their churches, but they forget that God can also work a miracle in their businesses. I want to remind you that God wants to work miracles in every part of your life, including in your business. Don't compartmentalize God out of your company.

I could offer you some theology here, some sound biblical teaching that might persuade you to believe that God can work a miracle in your business. But you probably already believe in miracles. You've been presented with this truth throughout your life as a believer. Yet somehow you refuse to apply your beliefs to your business. So instead, I want to offer you some real-life stories from my experience as a Christian CEO. God has shown me His miracle-working power more than once!

We were struggling financially a number of years ago, and I felt we might go bankrupt. Our cash flow was very tight, and I couldn't see a way through the predicament. I decided to travel to Dallas, Texas, to seek the advice and prayer of a dear friend, another Christian CEO. We were sitting together at breakfast when a woman suddenly sat down at our table. We'd never met her before, and she didn't claim to know me. She looked at me and stated that she saw me in her prayers and that the Lord had given her words just for me. I was, of course, surprised and a little skeptical. But here's what she told me: *"God has heard your cry. God is going to take care of your company. And finally, you will soon experience record-breaking sales and profits."*

Again, this woman didn't even know I owned a company or that I was also a believer. She asked us to bow our heads in prayer, which we did, and then after we lifted our heads, she disappeared. I looked all over for her in the restaurant, but I never saw her again. I believe this was a miracle, an angelic experience. Guess what happened? God did take care of our company. We didn't go bankrupt, and indeed we soon experienced record-breaking sales! I remember weeping when this dear woman prayed for me, and today, many years later, I still weep and rejoice when I recall this experience.

Years later, I was in prayer while exercising on a treadmill. We were struggling a bit once again, and I was praying for direction. Fortunately, we were not in a desperate situation, but even still, we needed a miracle to turn things around. As I prayed, I felt a strong sense from the Lord that He was going to perform another miracle.

Later that day, I received a phone call from a stranger, a man I'd never met before and didn't know existed. He informed me that his business, which was similar to ours, needed to be sold and that he wanted to sell it to me! He explained that he too was a believer and that he had been observing us from afar. For personal reasons, he felt it was time to sell and that God directed him to sell it to us. I was so astounded by God's grace in this situation. I wasn't even considering a purchase, but everything lined up so perfectly, and it was what we needed to break through another tough time.

Sometimes we don't need more theology or another sermon to be inspired to believe. Sometimes we need to hear it first-hand from another believer. So I'm telling you to start believing that God can work a miracle in your business.

18

DON'T ISOLATE YOURSELF

T HERE'S AN OLD adage, "It's lonely at the top." I can personally attest
to this feeling, both as a CEO and especially as a Christian CEO.
Many CEOs and other senior executives I've talked to tell me that one of
their biggest challenges is that they lack someone to talk to about their
toughest challenges. Leaders know they are ultimately responsible for
their organizations, and the well-being of many people rests in their hands.
If they fail, it affects the lives of many people, and it becomes a source of
embarrassment. A recent survey of CEOs by *Inc.* magazine revealed that
60 percent of all CEOs report feeling lonely and that it hindered their
performance. Frankly, I think the number is much higher.

When lonely and isolated, leaders eventually make bad decisions. They
sometimes even resort to alcohol or other addictions or risky behavior,
and they can become depressed and anxiety-ridden. Their relationships
with family and friends can break down, and eventually their world can
implode. Those leaders who are Christians and who aspire to live lives of
high integrity can also find it difficult to release or express these frustrations, and they also can go down the same destructive paths. We've heard
or read about some of these leaders, and it becomes very disappointing.

I have found that understanding why it can be so lonely at the top is the first step in developing better ways to manage these feelings and even avoid them altogether. Even accepting that you're isolated can help you climb out. I learned this lesson in a surprising way, and it helped me acknowledge and overcome feelings of being lonely at the top before I crashed. I'm grateful for how the Lord helped me discover a way out. Let me explain.

My business was booming, and I wanted to expand from Houston where I founded my business to the Dallas metro area. I talked to my staff about it, and everyone seemed excited and on board with the idea. So I pushed on with my expansion plans, despite how it was increasing my stress and challenging the business in other ways. I told a close friend about it. He's also the CEO of a growing business, and he persuaded me to join a small private group of Christian CEOs who meet regularly to discuss their business challenges and pray together. I accepted his invitation, and I'm so glad I did!

After opening up with the group and sharing my expansion plans, each of the CEOs advised me to rethink my plans. I was surprised at their resistance to my ideas, but I listened carefully to their advice. They asked me if I already dominated the Houston market. "No, I had not," I admitted to them. They challenged me to rethink about why I was going to spend so much money on the Dallas market when I hadn't even won the Houston market yet. I didn't have a good answer for them. I think my pride got in the way, and after we all prayed together, I realized that I was making decisions on my own, without the guidance and counsel of other believers.

When I later returned to my office, I informed my staff of how and why I changed my mind. To my utter amazement and surprise, they all told me they agreed with me! I was confused because my staff seemed so supportive of my Dallas expansion, but they now admitted to me that they thought it was a bad idea in the first place. When pressed to explain this to me, they said, "You seemed so excited about it, and we wanted to be supportive." This is when I realized how isolated I had become. I had built walls around myself and my position, to the point where my own team couldn't be honest with me.

I almost learned a lesson the hard way. But God intervened and sent me a group of Christian CEOs who to this day I still confide in and pray with. If you're feeling lonely and isolated, you can find freedom from the frustrations simply by getting together with others who are facing similar challenges. Your lonely feelings are to a large degree a self-fulfilling prophecy. The way out is easier than you might believe.

19

IT'S ALL IN THE EXECUTION

AFTER GRADUATION FROM seminary, I attended Harvard Business School where I learned a lot about managing a business. But for all the benefits of attending a business school, even one of the best, I can honestly say that I was not educated to execute. Business school curriculum, in my view, often fails to impart the useful and tactical skill of execution. Business theory is one thing, but when it comes to day-to-day management, it takes a lot more than theory to succeed. Business school professors use a scientific approach, using data to test a hypothesis by applying such tools as regression analysis. Instead of entering the real world of business, professors deal with simulations. In some instances, simulations are useful, necessary, and enlightening. But they often fail to reflect the way business works in real life.

Jesus was the master executor. He started with Himself and twelve disciples. They took to local villages, and then He saved the world! He didn't deal with theories or esoteric knowledge. What Jesus did was all about executing God's purposes for His life, death, and resurrection. Consider some of the ways Jesus executed His mission:

- He placed relationships above short-term or selfish gains.

- He found ways to accomplish goals by developing the potential of others.

- He believed in people, even when they don't believe in themselves.

- He gave clear feedback, praise, and rebuke when necessary.

- He was innovative and inspiring to others, bringing new ideas, new teaching, and creative solutions.

- He communicated in simple terms that even a child could understand.

Even before Jesus traveled to Jerusalem before His crucifixion, He gave specific and executable instructions to His disciples. I believe CEOs should also focus on execution if they are to be successful. Many do not, and they pay the price down the line. Many businesses don't make it past their second or third year because the owners don't think specifically about how to execute their vision and mission.

What does it mean to execute your business? How do you get past the ideation and creation stage? I've discovered four areas that, if implemented, will help you be a better executer. Ask yourself and your team these questions and then answer them. If you do, you'll be on your way to better execution.

Are your goals specific? Too often, CEOs are better at dreaming big than thinking small. But to achieve big dreams, you have to think specific. Break down your dreams into targeted and specific goals. A big vision is great, but it won't take you to where you want to go, without smaller, incremental steps.

Who's in charge of the goal? Who is going to execute it? Don't assume too much here. You and your team need to know specifically who's responsible for what. If you assume someone else is in charge, and that person assumes you're in charge, it's very possible nobody will be. Chart out at every step who is tasked with the details of reaching your goals.

What is the timeline? Although we'd all like to reach our goals tomorrow, you know it will take longer than you think. I find this area to be particularly frustrating to CEOs. We all want instant gratification and success by tomorrow! So take time to think through and plan your timelines. Be aggressive, but be reasonable. If you don't think about time, time will soon get away from you.

Finally, ask yourself how you're going to measure your progress. You can't monitor what you can't measure. Every CEO needs to assign measurable metrics and key indicators to every aspect of the business. How will you know otherwise if you're successful or not? For my part, I spend a great deal of time with my team discussing specific ways to measure our progress. This also helps the staff members better understand what's expected of them.

Don't wander aimlessly through your business. I love to dream big, and it's a good thing to be trained and educated in business, but like Jesus, who also focused on his day-to-day ministry, we as CEOs need to spend more time on the lost art of execution.

20

BE GENEROUS

WE STRIVE TO be a very generous company. We donate half of our profits to charitable causes, ministry, and other local and even national outreach organizations. Sometimes other CEOs will reach out to me and commend me for my actions and also tell me they also plan for their companies to become generous when they get to a certain revenue point. I sometimes challenge them to do it NOW, because if they aren't, I doubt they ever will. An entrepreneur once told me he planned to become generous when he hit one million dollars in revenue. I told him if you wait that long, you will never become a generous person. Generosity should be an urgent matter for you and your company! Be faithful in the little.

Matthew 6:33 says, "But seek ye first the kingdom of God and his righteousness, and all these things shall be added unto you." Did you get that? It all belongs to God. Nothing you own belongs to you. I learned this lesson early in my life, even before I became an entrepreneur, so when I founded our company, it had already been ingrained in my spirit. I didn't have to convince myself otherwise. This is not true for many people, and maybe not for you, so I want to show you how and why this is true.

The most important principle to keep firmly in mind is to understand whose money you are dealing with. The money you bring in and that goes out, your revenue and expenses, is God's. God's ownership of everything is a foreign concept to most of us. We like to think of our money and our possessions. Yet the Bible makes it clear that God owns everything:

For in him all things were created: things in heaven and on earth, visible and invisible, whether thrones or powers or rulers or authorities; all things have been created through him and for him. (Colossians 1:16)

To the Lord your God belongs the heavens, even the highest heavens, the earth and everything in it. (Deuteronomy 10:14)

For every animal of the forest is mine, and the cattle on a thousand hills. (Psalm 50:10)

The world is mine, and all that is in it. (Psalm 50:12)

"The silver is mine and the gold is mine," declares the LORD Almighty. (Haggai 2:8)

The money is all God's. If you allow Him to do so, He will use you as His vessel of blessing. He created you to be a blessing, and unless you submit yourself and your money to Him, I'm afraid that you won't be. I can say without hesitation that there is no greater feeling than seeing God work through you to bless others. Generosity is an important part of this.

Generosity is also the only true antidote to greed. At its heart, greed is simply the compulsion to take instead of give. Greed wants to own, hoard, and control. To escape greed, we have to reverse this evil heart attitude, and the best way to escape greed is to start giving. Do it today!

Like any antidote, giving is like a drug, and it can become addictive. Once you start giving, you will want to give more because it feels so good and it honors God. You'll eagerly look for more opportunities to bless other people. Before you know it, you're hooked on giving. Just as an addictive drug changes your brain, giving changes your heart!

21

WIN-WIN NEGOTIATION

WHEN I FIRST started to negotiate with vendors, suppliers, and others, my approach was to win by all means. I was an aggressive negotiator. This is not to say I was unfair and certainly not unethical, but still my tactics looked more like warfare than a talk at the peace table. I would also walk into a negotiation somewhat blind—blind to my own intentions and my end goal for the negotiation. I simply wanted to win.

Sometimes negotiating became somewhat hostile, but I mistakenly thought this was just a part of the process. I quickly found that this approach didn't always help me win, and in fact, sometimes I was the loser even if I got what I wanted in the short-term. The problem was that some of our relationships with vendors suffered because of my overly aggressive approach. Also, sometimes I'd "win" a negotiation without understanding why I was bartering in the first place. My ego would get ahead of me, and the end result did nothing to help my top or bottom line. I was winning just to feel good about my negotiating skills, not because it helped my company. Honestly, it became a form of greed, which is unbiblical.

I finally learned how to approach negotiating with a win-win attitude. To my surprise, not only did I get better pricing and terms, but when everyone at the table felt that they won, my relationships also improved and I had a much clearer understanding of why I was negotiating in the first place. I went from a win-lose approach to a win-win approach. Let me explain why this is a better approach for your business and how this is the way Jesus would negotiate.

If you think about negotiation as "getting your own way," "driving a hard bargain," or "beating the opposition," chances are you are sacrificing short-term gains for long-term losses. While you may win, the other side loses, and the outcome can damage your future relationships. It increases the likelihood of the relationship completely breaking down, of people walking out or refusing to deal with you ever again, and of the process ending in a bitter dispute. When you take an extreme position, such as asking the other side for much more than they expect to get, it is essentially dishonest because you're hiding your real views and misleading them about what you truly need out of the negotiation.

But when you approach a negotiation as a win-win, everyone literally comes out a winner. The goal is not to "beat" the other party, but to find a solution that everyone can feel good about. This doesn't mean that you must give up more than you should. You definitely need a clear picture of what you expect out of every negotiation. But it does mean that most people have an underlying need to feel good about themselves and will strongly resist any attempt at negotiation that might damage their self-esteem. Your aim should be to find some way of enabling both sides to feel good about themselves, while at the same time not losing sight of what you need.

Here's how you can better approach your negotiations as a win-win, not a win-lose.

First, have an open hand, meaning that you should know ahead of time that you can walk away. This is an important part of the process and is certainly better than becoming hostile. Walking away from the negotiating table can be polite and respectful. It shows the other party that you seriously understand what you want and need. You can't walk away successfully if you don't know what your goals are, so don't go in blindly. Be fully informed and prepared to know when you need to walk away, and then do so with respect. You'll be surprised at how the other party may respond, as he gets a clearer picture of what you need to work with him.

Then you need to explore and understand what your best alternative is to no deal, also referred to as BATNA. If you don't have an option B, you're going to lose either way. It also gives you a strong edge as the other side will know you have viable alternatives, which will make them more willing to deal. The problem is, in most high-stakes negotiations, there's really no viable alternative to a deal with the other party. There's no plan B, which means you're flying blind. But if you have a viable alternative that the other party is aware of, and you feel good about, it puts you in the driver's seat.

I love how the Bible gives us an example of godly negotiating. Remember when Moses negotiated with Pharaoh? Pharaoh did not agree initially, but he did continue to engage Moses. In fact, he responded negatively to Moses more than twenty times, before, during, and even after the plagues God sent. Yet Moses never changed his stated request of Pharaoh. He approached Pharaoh with firmness, respect, and in prayer and God's supernatural power. He also knew what he needed out of the negotiation. If Moses had asked only once for his people to be free, they would never have been freed. If he had given up and accepted the first few offers, they would never have been freed. Even if he had accepted the merciful offer to release the Israelites but without giving them any way to sustain themselves, they likely would have died in the desert. In the end, Moses stayed firm in his request, both stated and implied, and by doing so, he led the people to "a land flowing with milk and honey."

We serve the same God that Moses did, so don't forget that God's same supernatural power is available to you as well!

22

HIRING THE BEST

WHEN JESUS WAS walking along the sea of Galilee, early in His earthly ministry, He called a group of fishermen to follow Him. Simon Peter; Andrew; and James and John, the sons of Zebedee, all gave up their lucrative jobs as fisherman because they were attracted to Jesus and the culture He was creating. The Bible says, "They immediately left the ship and their father, and followed him."

As a CEO, I believe there's a lot to learn from how and when Jesus called His disciples, particularly in terms of how we recruit, train, and compensate our own teams. I'm reminded of a job interview and job offer I made to a new team member. This particular candidate was making significantly more money than I could offer her, and I knew it going into the interview. I made an offer anyway because I liked the candidate and I hoped she might accept. I was pleasantly surprised when she accepted the offer, but I was even more surprised at what she told me. "It wasn't all about the money," she said. It turned out she was more interested in my company's culture than the compensation I could offer.

I learned a valuable lesson, the same lesson that Jesus taught us. People will follow me and work for me, not solely because of how much money I can pay them, but also because of how much they enjoy their work at my company. It's about culture, not money. It's important for people to be able to bring their full selves to work. As people's work and personal lives become more intertwined than ever before, there is an increased expectation that team members enjoy their work and share values with their coworkers. The degree of comfort an individual team member feels at work is as important, I believe, as his compensation.

Benjamin Laker at *Forbes*[1] magazine studied corporate culture. His research concluded that companies with strong and positive corporate cultures have seen a fourfold increase in revenue growth. So not only are team members happier and recruitment easier, but your company will also grow faster. Laker says a good corporate culture is a company's single most powerful advantage, even more than compensation.

Yes, it's important to compensate staff in a fair and reasonable manner. But small to midsize companies cannot always afford to pay top-level salaries. We can, however, create a culture that values team members and makes their work enjoyable. For our company, we work hard to create an environment that values "joy" and "celebration." We work hard but have fun while we work. We offer generous vacation time and seven-hour work days, and we throw a lot of celebrations! As a result, we're able to recruit and retain top-quality staff.

Corporate culture is more than a buzzword. It's a principle Jesus valued as He recruited followers for His ministry. Jesus didn't offer compensation when He called his followers. Instead, He said, "I am the bread of life; whoever comes to me shall not hunger, and whoever believes in me shall never thirst." As CEOs and business leaders, we can also offer our team members a better "life" by building an environment that values people. This is something larger corporations cannot compete with, and it allows us to grow our businesses without breaking the bank.

23

BUILDING YOUR TEAM

I GREW UP IN a family business and watched my parents work very hard. They did absolutely everything including sales, marketing, shipping, customer service, and more. Just the two of them worked from sunrise to sunset, which made for a profitable business. The problem was that their business stagnated. It was a well-run and profitable business, but because they had little help, they lacked the ability to grow their business. It was a healthy, profitable, but small business.

There's certainly nothing wrong with running a small business with a small staff. Many business owners do just that, and it provides a steady source of income for the owners. But if you want to grow your business and earn greater profits and income, you have to get to the point where you can't try to do everything by yourself. You need a team to get it done. It's all about the team!

Even Jesus had a team. Think about that. Jesus was God incarnate. He possessed supernatural miracle power and could have literally done anything and everything by Himself. Instead, He chose a team of twelve disciples whom He trained, supported, and ultimately commissioned to take over and manage His mission on earth. He didn't just pick the team and leave it at that. He took the time to give them instructions. He invested in them, teaching them and taking them along wherever He went. And Jesus seldom did ministry by Himself. He always ministered with the disciples nearby. In fact, the Bible indicates that He usually had at least three disciples with Him wherever He went. In the sense that Jesus was all-powerful and could do whatever He wanted, He did not need a ministry team, but He built one, which I believe is an important lesson for us.

One of the hardest decisions you'll ever make as a CEO and business owner is knowing when to add to your team. Even that very first hire, the one you make after hiring yourself, is a tough one. You have confidence in yourself and your own abilities. You also know that people are expensive, and as soon as you hire someone new, you have to pay him. It's a new fixed expense that you can't get out of unless you fire someone. So it's a scary time for any business owner.

But the problem is that if you don't begin to build a team, your business is also in danger. It will sit there in limbo as you work hard but don't see the fruits of your labor. So despite it being risky to hire and build a team, the same is true if you don't. In fact, I can promise you that if you don't build a team, there is no way you're going to grow your business. When you reach capacity within your business, you cannot take on more clients, do more for current clients, or get your products in more locations. You become limited in your reach and in your potential because more cannot be done. The revenue you are losing could end up being more than the cost of hiring the right help to assist with the increased workload. When you add the right staff at the right time, you have the potential to keep expanding your business.

Let me encourage you to have the faith in God and his business to invest in building a great team. Take some time to assess your workload, the skills of the existing staff (if you have any), your budget relative to future potential, and your overall goals to reach new heights in revenue and profit. Yes, there is always a cost to bring on a new team member. You can expect your profit and loss to take a hit at the beginning. How long it will be before you start seeing profits from the expanded staff depends on the company. It may be a month, it may be three, or it may be longer. So faith is required. Look at this as an opportunity to grow in your faith. I can tell you from experience that it will always be a leap of faith. But team-building is something Jesus was very good at, and you can trust that He will help you do what He did.

24

TRUST YOUR TEAM

NEARLY EVERY CEO I advise and coach thinks that he is the smartest one in the room. He sees himself as his company's top advisor, lead problem-solver, and thinker-in-chief. Do you see yourself as the sharpest and most intelligent person in your organization? Be honest with me (and with yourself).

If your answer is "yes" or even "maybe," then you have a problem that you are probably blind to. Let me be straight with you: You're not the smartest person in your organization. Thinking that you are, and that you personally need to drive every idea for your team, is not only unrealistic but also exhausting. It's why you feel burned out sometimes. It's a self-induced burden.

Leaders with this attitude eventually become more obsessed with dreaming up the next great solution or idea rather than focusing on team development. When this happens, the leader becomes a silo and the team stops contributing with honesty. It gives the team members a free pass: "The boss has it all handled, so why should we come up with anything?" Eventually, the burden is too big to handle and the organization itself becomes so top-heavy, it crumbles under itself.

What's smarter and more sustainable is to hire people who are smarter than you, and also to give up on your ego. You have to learn to trust the people you hired. If you can't get past yourself and trust your team, you're going to be in the middle of your own mess, with only yourself to blame. The Bible says, "When pride comes, then comes disgrace, but with humility comes wisdom" (Proverbs 11:2). I've learned that the fastest way for CEOs to create new ideas, fix problems, and grow their organizations is to hire people who are smarter than they are and to build effective teams and rely on them to do the hard work. It's not easy at first, especially if you're the company's founder and the ONLY original team member. But eventually you need to transition yourself away from soloist to choir director.

Have you ever wondered how Jeff Bezos[2] rose from obscurity to the CEO of one of the world's biggest and fastest-growing organizations? Bezos, Amazon founder and CEO, once paid a visit to the headquarters of Basecamp. During an open Q&A session, he commented on what he thought made the smartest leaders. It's not the answer you'd expect. Bezos said the smartest leaders are those who change their minds along the way, finding new information, revisiting their knowledge, finding holes in their own proposed solutions, and staying open to new ideas and to those who **challenge their viewpoint**. In other words, they never assume they have all the answers.

But let's also look to Jesus as our example, the world's greatest CEO. There's no question that Jesus WAS the smartest in the room, right? Yet He spent three years building trust with His team, His disciples—not as a micromanager but as a team builder. He allowed them to be honest, vulnerable, and to ask such questions as "Who is the greatest among us?" He fell asleep in a boat during a crisis, postponed a trip to Judea while his friend Lazarus lay sick and died, and watched as Peter sliced off the ear of a Roman soldier. He let them make their own mistakes, find their own way, and learn to trust God as their problem solver.

Just as Jesus did, once you learn to ask the right questions that will bring out thoughtful, manageable ideas from team members and the more they own them, the more they will try harder to see their ideas work. The biggest revelation I can give you is that you don't need to come up with ALL the wisdom, insight, and creative output. Learn to make disciples, not robots, and commission them to take your product or services to the world. When you start to trust your team, they'll learn to trust you, and the end result will be a stronger team and company.

25

CELEBRATE YOUR TEAM

I'VE MET VERY few CEOs who tell me they have a plan to celebrate their team, either as a group or individually, and I also know of very few companies that place "celebration" at the forefront of their corporate values. We have dared to be different in this area, and I want to share with you why and how it's helped us create a healthier culture and a more profitable company.

We take the Bible's admonition "the joy of the Lord is your strength" (Nehemiah 8:10) very seriously, and in a very fun way! When Ezra said, "The joy of the Lord is your strength," he was speaking to the remnant of Israel who had returned to Judah to rebuild the city and its temple. It was a time of restoration, not only of the ruined city, but also of obedience to the law of God. The people were filled with sorrow and weeping when they heard God's law and realized how far they had gone away from its teaching. But Ezra told them to rejoice and celebrate because they were going to build it back.

In a similar way, as we build our company, we encourage our team members to celebrate and be joyful. In fact, it's a part of our core values. We designate several team members to manage it, just as we have designated team members to manage every other department in our company. Why do we place so much importance on creating a fun and happy workplace? Why is celebration a fixture in our corporate culture?

Have you noticed that the world has become a depressing place? Negativity, isolationism, sadness, and anxiety are pervasive in our culture. As a follower of Jesus, it's important to remember all the reasons we have to be joyful, just as the Bible does. So when someone walks into our business, whether as a part of the team or not, we want him to feel the joy of the Lord. We don't want people to walk into a Christian company and to feel the same way that they feel outside. We want them to feel joy. So our workplace is determined not to be a part of our negative world. We brim with optimism and positivity.

Our positive workplace culture improves teamwork, raises morale, increases productivity and creativity, lowers turnover, and most importantly, reduces stress. All of this helps us build a company that can grow and be more profitable. But this is not the reason we do it. They are all positive consequences, but we do it because we are followers of Jesus. We have so much to be joyful about, even when the world around us seems so unhappy. Jesus is Lord! So even if our celebrations did nothing to help us build our company and make us more profitable, we are joyful in our salvation and know that we will spend eternity with Jesus.

I encourage you to take a close look at whether or not your company celebrates with its team members. I don't mean the occasional birthday cake or meeting where you recognize a team member for a job well done. Most companies do that. I mean that you should *plan* to celebrate, making it a part of your company's process and procedure. Be intentional and consistent about it. Be strategic in a way that everyone on your team, and even outsiders, know that your company is a joyful one.

We formed a three-person celebration team, led by a loving and caring team member who loves to spread the joy of the Lord. This team meets regularly to decide when, how, and who to celebrate. New team members complete a questionnaire (see below), sharing some personal preferences that help us create custom celebrations for personal days (for example, birthdays and anniversaries) and for reaching professional milestones at work. We curate the fun intentionally, not in an accidental or occasional way.

Over the years, we've organized some amazing celebrations that are remembered and talked about. We once brought a party to a remote worker, one of our veteran team members of sixteen years who could not leave his home. It was a huge event attended by most of our staff, right there in the front yard of the team member. The joy of the Lord was so present that tears were shed. Not only was the celebration greatly appreciated by the team member himself, but it also provided an opportunity for the entire team to display God's love corporately. We could feel the presence of the Lord in our midst.

For some CEOs, creating a fun and celebratory culture might seem to be a trivial thing. But take it from this CEO, you will not regret the benefits you'll reap both personally and professionally.

Below is our company's questionnaire for new team members. We use this list to personalize each celebration gift for each team member. They are always touched by the intentional celebration and customized gift.

1. Favorite color?

2. Favorite flower?

3. Favorite hot beverage?

4. Favorite cold beverage?

5. Favorite snack item?

6. Favorite candy?

7. Favorite hobby/things to do outside of work?

8. Favorite website(s):

9. Favorite magazine, author, and/or type of book?

10. Favorite movie/type of movie?

11. Favorite music/singing artist? Pop/Country/Love Songs.

12. Favorite local restaurant?

13. Favorite place to shop?

14. Other favorites: Dessert:

15. Birthdate and other significant dates (month and day only):

16. Spouse's name:

17. Children's name(s):

18. Type of pets/names:

26

CREATE A FUN CULTURE

ALL WORK AND no play will likely lead to less productive, dissatisfied workers. So if you're a driven CEO who has trouble pausing to celebrate and have plain good fun, think again. Your seriousness won't necessarily move your team members to work harder, but instead to work less. I've seen this happen time and time again when I visit other companies, even those owned and operated by Christian CEOs. Owners sometimes forget that it takes work to have fun. You have to find intentional ways to lighten the atmosphere and make the drudgery of work fun for everyone on your team. Why?

Besides making working lives more enjoyable, there is actually evidence that fun in the workplace packs a powerful punch in terms of organizational benefits. For example, a study by John Michel from Loyola University and Michael Tews from Penn State University[3] found that workers who socialized more in the workplace and who saw their coworkers and the workplace as more fun were less likely to leave. Fun in the workplace can also foster more positive attitudes, reduce stress, energize people, and help teams become more cohesive while they develop stronger relationships with each other. In addition, fun makes people more creative because it allows them to think playfully. Being playful without being limited by fear of failure can give your team a huge boost of creativity.

It's also biblical to have fun. Ecclesiastes 2:4 says, "There is nothing better for a person than that he should eat and drink and find enjoyment in his toil. This also, I saw, is from the hand of God." It doesn't get any more direct than that! So finding ways to have fun at work is something God actually commands. Even Jesus hints at having fun. There are some direct clues about Jesus' joyfulness, so we might infer His laughter. The most obvious is Luke 10:21: "At that time Jesus, full of joy through the Holy Spirit, said, 'I praise you, Father, Lord of heaven and earth, because you have hidden these things from the wise and learned, and revealed them to little children. Yes, Father, for this was your good pleasure.'"

We rewrote the script for fun at work! Experiment in your workplace, get creative, laugh out loud, and encourage everyone to have some fun. You don't have to be Zappos, Google, or Facebook to build fun into your culture. Well-placed humor in an office environment puts others at ease. It raises energy, encourages innovation, and undoubtedly improves productivity. I've been known to tell my team to go home early to get ready for the Super Bowl and to order every appetizer on the menu when taking my staff to lunch. These are things our team remembers years later. We celebrate birthdays, anniversaries, weddings, and new babies. The time we take off to have fun and celebrate is easily made up for by happy team members.

I've also discovered that some of our best ideas sprout not from official meetings and memos, but from casual experiences among team members. It seems that when everyone's guard is down, the ideas start to flow.

But here's what's really important: Your team members are also likely to value fun in the workplace more highly if you, your managers, and team leaders are supportive of fun. In simple terms, it is the difference between a manager who, as everyone runs to the break room to have birthday cake, signals "Great, let's all go and celebrate and then we will get back to work," and one that mutters "Here we go again; people are going to get distracted and we will lose thirty minutes of work time." Fun cannot be faked. It has to be genuine and sincere, from the heart. Your team will notice if you're manufacturing fun instead of enjoying it.

27

TEAM MEMBER INSTEAD OF EMPLOYEE

ONE OF MY personal convictions, going back to when I launched out as a business owner and entrepreneur, is not to use the word "employee." Instead I've always referred to my staff as "team members." It might sound trite at first glance, but we take it very seriously, and it's become an embedded part of our organization. We were calling each other team members before it was cool to do so! You might do the same, but are you doing so with intention? Does your team feel like a team? You might think that there's not much difference between the two, a matter of mere semantics. But I say there's a world of difference.

There are quite a few valid reasons not to call (and treat) your people as employees. I'll get into that soon, but first and foremost, as a Christian CEO, I follow the example of Jesus, who was a servant-leader. Jesus was unconcerned with titles, organizational charts, and hierarchy. During a time of crisis, even though He was worthy of being worshiped as King, He washed the feet of His disciples, including the one who would betray Him (John 13:1–17). Jesus chose a towel and basin, not a job title, to define how He served His team. He showed us that foot washing, not power taking, is the way of the Gospel.

What does this mean for your company or organization? For instance, if you have employees, you likely don't have dedicated, committed workers. Employees work for a paycheck. They clock in and clock out. They don't work for you; they work for the money. They don't work for your customer; they work for the money. They will likely leave you when someone up the road offers them a bigger paycheck. They rarely go the extra mile unless it means more money. Of course, there is nothing wrong with staff wanting to make money, but if money is the primary reason someone works for you, money will also be the reason they stop working for you.

Team members, on the other hand, are dedicated and loyal to you and to the organization, and they feel a sense of ownership in their work. It's not just about the paycheck. If your people need you to tell them what to do every step of the way, then you have employees. Team members take initiative, seek out opportunities to contribute, and don't wait to be given directives. Employees do the work that's assigned to them, but that's where it ends. If you have employees, you might be lucky to get compliance, but with team members, you have true commitment.

Team members also tend to share their ideas, while employees share complaints. Team members work together, not against each other. Employees become over-focused on protecting what they perceive to be their "turf," rather than directing energy toward collaboration. Because of this, they become task-oriented, checking off items on a list, rather than working collectively to achieve big-picture goals. Team members, on the other hand, share goals and try to come together in unison to achieve an organization's mission.

Teams don't require titles and managers; they need leaders who don't hand down orders, but rather work alongside them. I'm a big believer in clear and well-defined job descriptions, but I've also learned how a good team has the mentality that everyone succeeds or fails as one. When one team member needs help, another team member will swoop in without needing to be asked to help. Teams will work together outside the confines of their individual job descriptions on behalf of each other, for the organization as a whole.

I always look to the Bible for guidance, not just for inspiration, but also to discover how to execute and implement. When team-building, I like to read the story of Nehemiah. God used Nehemiah to build a team of people ready to serve and sacrifice alongside Him. Having assessed the work ahead of him, Nehemiah cast the vision God had given to him in Persia. He spoke of the great need ("Jerusalem lies in ruins") and painted a picture of a godly and glorious future ("that we may no longer suffer derision"). Then he proclaimed, "You see the trouble **we** are in, how Jerusalem lies in ruins with its gates burned. Come, let **us** build the wall of Jerusalem, that we may no longer suffer derision" (Nehemiah 2:17–18).

There are many ways to create and build your team, not just a group of "workers." I encourage you to use the example Jesus gave us, and the many examples of team-building in the Bible, to do what we did and grow an organization of people who care for each other and our customers!

28

SHOUT OUTS!

OUR COMPANY IS famous for our "shout outs." Every day, we set aside time for encouragement, compliments, praise, and prayer. It's an important part of our day, and I'll explain how and why.

Successful CEOs understand that one of the keys to a healthy organization is to build a corporate culture based on a shared set of beliefs and values that are supported by both strategy and structure. When an organization has a strong culture, then its team members know how to respond to any given situation, and they understand how they will be rewarded for demonstrating the organization's values. Conversely, the lack of a strong culture can tear down the organization and its leadership. It will lead to disengaged employees who treat customers poorly, to high turnover, and to chaotic internal communication, all of which will negatively impact your bottom line.

If you're reading this and you feel that you need to breathe new life into your company culture, it's going to take some work. You can start by asking:

- Do your team members enjoy their work? Their work should not bring a feeling of dread.

- Are your team members engaged? They should feel that they are listened to.

- Is there accountability and responsibility? Taking ownership makes team members feel connected.

- Is there a sense of camaraderie and respect? People like to be needed.

- How do you invest in your team members? Giving recognition shows that you value their work.

You, as CEO, have a vital role in perpetuating a strong culture based on the Bible, starting with recruiting and selecting applicants who will thrive in your culture, but even more so, in creating ways to sustain your culture on a daily basis. You have to find ways to live your God-led culture every day. You also must go out of your way to communicate your cultural identity to team members as well as prospective new hires. You need to be clear about your values and how those values define your organization and determine how your organization is run. This is why we do it.

There are many ways to create and build your corporate culture. One way is to make sure your team understands your mission statement, vision statement, and shared values. But I decided many years ago that it needs to be more than simply reading aloud our mission and vision statements. It needs to involve a committed daily task of culture-building. There are many forces fighting against you, particularly if you've placed Jesus at the helm of your company. So culture-building cannot be irregular or inconsistent. It has to be strategic, tactical, and consistent. Culture is a nebulous concept, an undefined aspect of your organization, so you have to make it intentional when doing it, and you have to put your people first. I believe that my people drive my organization's performance and productivity. So here's what we do.

Every morning at 10:00, the entire company puts its work on pause to gather together corporately in a time of positive reflection and applause. Maybe we don't literally applaud each other (although sometimes we do!), but it's time for all of us to tell each other why and how we're doing a great job. It's a time for management to express a grateful heart, for staff members to thank each other, and for us to remind each other how each individual is important. We end in prayer, thanking God for His greatness, and asking for His continued guidance and discernment.

When I started doing this daily, some thought it might serve as a distraction. But on the contrary, my team members soon looked forward to the time together. It bonded us together and served as a constant reminder that our corporate culture embodied the love and joy of Christ. I've learned a lot from my team during this time. Our communication is honest and straightforward. When we freely offer our support for each other, people are also more apt to offer constructive advice in areas where we are weak.

However you create and build your company's culture, make sure to carve out some time for everyone to bond, fellowship, and give compliments. You'll be grateful you did!

29

CELEBRATE RESIGNATIONS

WHEN JESUS PROPHESIED that Peter would deny Him three times, He didn't in turn deny or renounce Peter. On the contrary, He loved Peter and soon afterwards prophesied, "And so I say to you, you are Peter, and upon this rock I will build my church, and the gates of the netherworld shall not prevail against it" (Matthew 16:18). Even Peter's abject denial did not move Jesus toward rejecting him.

As an owner and CEO, I remind you of this story from the Bible in terms of your own team members who leave you. It's never easy to see staff go. When they resign or otherwise leave your company, it's very easy to take it personally. The conversation usually goes like this: "I've decided to take a job offer at another company." Suddenly you feel as if you were punched in the stomach. And then, instead of recovering in a few minutes, the shock and pain slowly turn into disappointment, anger, and dread. You try to take it easy and be congenial with your staff member, but inside you're hurt.

This took me a while to work and pray through. But I've learned (the hard way) how to deal with staff members who quit. Today we literally

CELEBRATE their resignations! That might sound like I've taken things too far, but let me explain to you how and why this is an important part of your company's health and stability.

First, you need to remember that as a founder, you willingly commit years of your life to working on a single goal: turning something you're passionate about into a growing business. You make a lot of sacrifices along the way. But you can't expect the same of literally anyone else who isn't a co-founder. Aside from you (and any other owners), staff members don't just work hard on your business. They work hard on **themselves**, and they are constantly working to better themselves and their position in life. While they share your goal for your business, their great goal is to better themselves. You need to keep this in mind.

Second, your people are God's people. They don't belong to you. God has a specific will for everyone's life, and God's will is not always that your people will be glued to you. You have to acknowledge that God may indeed desire for your staff, even key and senior staff, to do His will elsewhere. If you feel that you own your people, instead of God, you're going to take resignations personally, which goes against God's will. Hold on to your people loosely as if God loaned them to you. Pray for them, each of them individually, that God will use them for His glory at your company OR somewhere else.

Finally, if Jesus is your CEO, you have to trust that no single person's resignation can negatively affect HIS company. Nobody is indispensable, and often when one person departs, it opens the doors to someone who God is ready to place in that person's stead "for such a time as this." I can't tell you how many times I was surprised by how quickly my company recovered from a key resignation. Other people will rise to the occasion because God placed them there. Remember it's HIS company, not yours.

So when a staff member leaves, celebrate his new opportunity. Take him to coffee or lunch, bring a cake to work and spread the joy, and show your team how much you trust Jesus! Your team members joined your team because they trusted you in the first place. You need to deliver on that trust all the way to the end, whether they're moving on to something else or not. When a team member leaves, your company will get over it. Wish that person well, and mean it. Because that's what you signed up for when you hired him.

30

PRODUCTIVE MEETINGS

I NTERNAL CORPORATE MEETINGS are the bane of corporate life. There are too many meetings, they take too long, and they get too little accomplished. We've all "been there." We sit through endlessly long meetings and leave them feeling tired, unaccomplished, and confused.

Even research confirms that most meetings are a waste of time. Professor Steven Rogelberg, an organizational psychologist at the University of North Carolina, wrote a book on the subject called *The Surprising Science of Meetings: How You Can Lead Your Team to Peak Performance.*[4] Through research, he ascertained that there are about 55 million business meetings across the country each day, and that when polled, more than 50 percent of the participants say that they are a complete waste of time. In fact, those who are most positive about meetings are the ones who lead them!

In my experience on both sides of the fence, as leader and as participant, I've discovered several consequences to poorly organized meetings:

- They often result in more work, not less work, for staff.

- A lack of clearly defined action steps leads to confusion.

- Bad meeting organization results in tension and even battles between staff members.

- Leaders develop poorer relationships with staff who detest their meetings.

This is an area I've homed in on and improved as an entrepreneur and CEO, and it's made a significant difference in how my business is run and in the morale of my team. During the early days of my business, I learned the hard way. But then I turned my meetings over to Christ.

What specifically did I change?

First, remember that sometimes meetings are really not necessary. Before you call a meeting, think about whether you can accomplish your goals through email or a quick phone call. You rarely need to call a meeting if you're just planning to share information or issue action instructions. You want to empower your team to get the job done, not waste time in meetings.

Then, be predictable. The worst thing you can do is for staff to show up at a meeting with no idea of what to expect. So I've learned to run all my meetings in a similar fashion, with Christ at the center. This is what I mean:

- Every meeting starts with prayer. This is a reminder to all of us, meeting leader and participants, that Jesus is at the center of every issue at our company.

- Every meeting includes a brief conversation about how everyone is doing, a time to share about what's going on in our lives. I take this time to encourage staff. This helps to reduce tension and brings the peace of Christ into our meetings.

- Then a brief time of celebration and congratulations for what's going RIGHT with the business. It's easy to get dragged down by problems, so I take time to talk about progress.

- By this time, meeting participants are relaxed and ready to creatively address the problems at hand. We tackle them one by one, cooperatively, and with succinct action steps. I ensure that everyone knows specifically what to do next. I also keep my door open for post-meeting conversations.

- Finally, we also end in prayer. Jesus is the Alpha and Omega, the beginning and end, of every decision at my company. So finding time to pray before and after our meetings keeps Him at the center.

It's impossible for every meeting to run completely smoothly. We are humans, and even the best of us have bad days. But if you strive for predictable, focused, and Christ-centered meetings, you'll get more done, and your staff will be all the happier for it.

31

HOW TO THINK ABOUT YOUR SALARY

YOUR SALARY, YOUR "take home" income, is something that every entrepreneur struggles with. If you're the only one deciding how much income you're going to earn, rather than your boss, then how much? Should you earn a high or low salary? Somewhere in the middle? I'm going to challenge you here in a way that might be contrary to popular opinion. I cannot argue that it's necessarily what God wants for you, or that He commands it. But I can argue that it would be the best thing for you and for your company.

First, you should be careful not to live extravagantly. Sometimes a highly successful CEO or entrepreneur literally raids his company's bank account to spend lavishly on himself and his family. They buy expensive houses and cars, and they take expensive vacations. This is, however, a dangerous precedent. I like how *The Message* shares about what Jesus says about living a lavish life in Luke 12:16–20:

Then he told them this story: *"The farm of a certain rich man produced a terrific crop. He talked to himself: 'What can I do? My barn isn't big enough for this harvest.' Then he said, 'Here's what I'll do: I'll tear down my barns and build bigger ones. Then I'll gather in all my grain and goods, and I'll say to myself, Self, you've done well! You've got it made and can now retire. Take it easy and have the time of your life!' Just then God showed up and said, 'Fool! Tonight you die. And your barnful of goods—who gets it?'"*

Did you get that? He literally calls the big spender a fool! I believe it's foolish on many levels to pay yourself an unreasonably high salary, even if your company is highly profitable. It will tempt you away from your responsibilities at your company, as you will spend more time thinking about ways to spend your money rather than to make more money. You'll also become despised by your own team, maybe even your friends, family, and those at church.

The Bible clearly tells us to be content with what we have. Hebrews 13:15 says, "Keep your life free from love of money, and be content with what you have, for he has said, 'I will never leave you nor forsake you.'" You won't be content with what you have if you keep on spending more and more money on material things such as fancy homes and cars. Instead of finding contentment, you'll literally want more and more. The secret to being content with what you have is to live modestly.

So when thinking about and planning for your salary, I challenge you to pay yourself somewhere in the middle. Don't pay yourself too much or too little. Pay yourself modestly. But what exactly does it mean to live a modest lifestyle? It's in the eye of the beholder. My definition of a modest lifestyle might look like living in poverty to some people. I'm sure others would view your lifestyle as luxurious. There is no biblical mandate for exactly what this means, but if you look around yourself and the people who are near to you, you will find the way. Living modestly usually means battling the motivations to spend. It often means taking a little more time to find what you need, and really, really, really wanting something before you buy it. And it means being willing to accept that what you already have is good enough.

You also don't want to pay yourself too little. If you're living poorly— struggling to pay your bills and to raise your family—you'll end up with a bitter attitude about your work and your company. If you struggle to make ends meet, you'll lose momentum and stop being excited about your work. So I don't recommend sacrificing so much that you start looking for a way out of what God wants you to do. There is nothing wrong with earning an income that is fulfilling and good for you and your family, in a modest way. As your company grows, you can make adjustments to your income, but even then, remember to put God first and avoid the temptation to spend rather than to serve.

32

PROCESS, PROCESS, PROCESS

EMERGING, UPSTART COMPANIES don't take the time to create and develop processes to keep their business growing, stable, healthy, and organized. They are consumed with creating products and services and selling them. This is to be expected, as the primary goal of a new business is simply to "make it." In fact, one of the keys to success is treating your new business like a baby. Just like an infant, your company needs constant attention at the beginning if you want it to be healthy and grow. It needs constant feeding and changing.

But as your company gets older and you become more experienced as a parent and entrepreneur, your company, like your child, will begin to sustain itself. The way that you manage your company then changes. Rather than focusing on birthing a new life, your job is to train, discipline, teach, and sustain. This means it's time to develop processes, because you can't be everywhere and do everything at once. Also, just as a parent helps his growing child learn to be safe, secure, and prudent, you need to do the same with your company. Again, this is achieved through the development of sound business processes and procedures.

The Bible says, "The heart of man plans his way, but the Lord establishes his steps" (Proverbs 16:9). This means as a CEO, you need to establish steps that guide your heart and your passions. It's easy as an entrepreneur to want to keep creating things rather than tend to processes and procedures, but the Bible clearly tells us to establish process (steps), which will be your company's guardrail as you grow.

The key reasons to have well-defined business processes include:

- To clearly Identify what tasks are important to your larger business goals across all spectrums, among all staff, and with all stakeholders.

- To clarify communication among your people, functions, teams, and departments.

- To ensure proper approvals to ensure accountability and not waste resources.

- To prevent chaos and confusion from creeping in to your day-to-day operations.

- To standardize a set of procedures to complete tasks that really matter to your business.

The arrival of COVID-19 was a rude awakening for business owners who were not prepared with processes and procedures. Of course, none of us could have predicted the sudden jolt to our businesses and economy—even to our personal lives. But for those companies that already had well-thought out processes, the transition was easier. As a CEO, part of your job is to think about and plan for the unexpected. Your role as CEO is partly to help develop a process and procedure for the unexpected emergencies that will eventually occur. It will not always be smooth sailing, and if you haven't learned that by now, you will!

When I say "business processes," what do I mean? A business process includes a combination of documented steps that are interlinked. Think of it as a written checklist of best practices and methods that sustain your business's operations, no matter who specifically is in charge. In other words, your business process guides your people, not the other way around. Good business process means that you aren't totally dependent on a specific person or people. At our company, we've developed a large "book," a written and well-document plan for every possible circumstance. The process also outlines how the business operates in finances, in human resources, in sales and marketing, in compliance with laws and regulations, and at every level of management. It's our internal operational "bible," and we update it regularly. It includes:

- HR processes, including team member recruitment, hiring, and benefits.

- Management responsibilities across all levels in the company.

- Capital management, reporting, and financial analysis.

- Product development processes.

- Customer acquisition and sales channel processes.

- Sales and marketing processes.

- Financial processes including receivables, payables, and cash flow.

- Service and product delivery processes.

- IT and related technology processes.

Yes, it takes a lot of time and work to think through and document your process. Large companies devote entire staff and teams to create and execute processes. If you're the CEO of a small- to medium-size company, you may want to hire a consultant or part-time resource to help you create your process and procedure. And remember, the Bible is your process guide. Jesus is your CEO, and He will help you create a process that is inspired by and based on the Word.

33

YOUR TRUE COMPETITION

WHEN WE STARTED our office supply company, we searched for and researched our competitors far and wide. We spent countless hours evaluating each of our competitors, which are many (Staples, Office Depot, etc.), and looking for our competitive advantages or disadvantages. I would say we were obsessed with it for some time. Then it struck me that our real competitors are not "out there." They are within. Let me explain.

Understanding who your competitors are and what they are doing can help your business, especially at the beginning when you're just getting your footing. But at the same time, your time is limited. Startups are intrinsically linked to very limited resources, and as your company's CEO or entrepreneur, your focus should be on developing your core vision, your mission, and your target customer base. If you're not sure who that is, then you're in trouble. But by putting your limited time and resources into figuring out what potential competitors are doing, you're actually ignoring your potential customers.

Also, you don't want to end up being a copycat and simply following the crowd rather than pursuing your own vision and mission. Startups are meant to be innovative, right? By definition, that means creating something new and different. Many CEOs I know spend too much time simply refining another company's product, service, or mission, rather than uniquely creating their own. If you do this, you'll suddenly find yourself with a mishmash of ideas from others rather than your own unique and tightly focused ideas based on who your customers are. You might literally end up copying a competitor who is targeting a completely different customer from you.

Who's your real competitor? You are! Your competition rests within you and your company. Rather than being outwardly focused, try focusing inward and search for those things within your company that are holding you back. I suspect in most cases, the real issue isn't the competition from others but from inside your own company. So try competing with yourself instead of others. Yes, business can be a competition, but the race that you face doesn't have to be against anybody else. A better way to refocus your efforts and harness competition is to look in the mirror and learn how to compete with yourself.

I recommend you look at three areas within your company and create ways to compete with yourself within them. Find ways to better create, sustain, and manage your goals to become excellent in these areas. Organizational excellence can be associated with sustained prosperity!

Is your company excellent in every way?

Work to ensure that every part of your company is run with excellence, not just in one department but in every one from accounting to human resources to customer service to sales and marketing. Sometimes a CEO is super focused on one single area but lacks the ability to look across the entire landscape of a company to assure excellence throughout. It's not good enough to be excellent at one thing. And if you can become excellent in every area, suddenly your competitors aren't the problem anymore.

Are you telling a strong brand story?

Every CEO and entrepreneur has a story to tell, whether it's how he founded their company, why he decided to enter an industry, or how he turned a passion project into a lucrative business. These narratives weave together into a brand story that resonates with your customers, vendors, and team members. It cultivates a community of brand advocates who stand behind and support you. The problem with focusing too much on your competitors is that you try to tell the wrong story—their story—instead of your own. But it's crucial to learn how to build your own brand story that's unique to you and your company.

How do your customers feel about you?

You are nothing without your customers. Whether or not you have competitors, the bottom line is that your business will live or die based on how and what your customers think about you.

Do you know what your customers think about your business? What is their view of the product or service they receive? Are you listening to your customers? Are you putting your customers first? Have you looked at your business from your customers' perspective? It is very easy to get caught up in what your competitors are doing and not put your customers first. We decided early on in our business to regularly ask our customers what they think about us. By doing so, we've been able to outsmart our competition without even realizing we were doing it.

As we read the gospels, we see Jesus never thought or talked about His competitors. He focused inwardly, not outwardly. He spent most of His time in public ministry focused on the heart: making disciples. Jesus made disciples who made disciples. Let that sink in! He didn't do so by asking His disciples to look at or think about the "competition." Nor should you.

34

KNOWING YOUR CUSTOMER

WHEN I READ and study my Bible, and something I've observed about Jesus and His healing ministry is that He was intentional about who He healed. He didn't heal everyone. In fact, He didn't heal many of the people He came into contact with. We don't know why Jesus chose to heal some people and not others, but we can surmise that He had reasons. His miracles were not random.

I think there's an important lesson here for business leaders. Not every customer is your customer. Your job, as CEO, is not to find ways to reach everyone. Your job is to strategically decide WHO your customers are, and then find ways to reach them.

This is one of the biggest mistakes I see other companies and organizations make. They try to be everything to everyone, thinking the goal is to sell, sell, sell. But in the process, they lose their way. They literally sacrifice their own core values and convictions to appease customers who eventually end up costing their companies' profits. Not every customer is a good customer.

Larry Seldon and Geoffrey Colvin wrote a classic breakthrough business book about this very thing, called *Angel Customers and Demon*

Customers: Discover Which is Which and Turbo-Charge Your Stock. They shared that one of the oldest myths in business is that every customer is a valuable customer. They show with research how many businesses don't realize that some of their customers are unprofitable, and that simply doing business with them is costing them money. I wholeheartedly agree, and I have been telling colleagues this very thing for years.

It's not always easy for a startup or younger company to send customers away, but even in infancy, it's a good idea to begin to think this way. As your company matures, you can begin the process of defining who your ideal customer is. While it's true that the customer is king, if you spread yourself too thin and treat every customer the same, you'll have too many kings! You can deliver a service right only if you have full information about your customer. This will help you in knowing how he likes things done and delivered. People are different and therefore have different preferences. Understanding this will help you in knowing how best to approach them.

An organization will win in wowing the customer if they took time to learn who their customer is.

For example, your company might sell a high-value product or service. If you do, but then you try to sell to customers who simply cannot afford your high-value product or service, you'll mistakenly look for ways to lessen the quality. You will sacrifice your company's core values just to make another sale. This approach will eventually damage your sales efforts to high-value customers. It's a vicious circle.

How do you define who your customer is? I spend time with our team, and we build processes of creating either a customer profile or customer persona that helps us clearly define our customers' needs by understanding their buying patterns, such as what, how, and where they buy, and more importantly, their motivations for buying. This process evolves over time and is not always constant. In other words, our defined customer can change as our company matures. That's to be expected. The important thing is to make the effort, to ensure that your entire company is intentionally selling to the kind of customer who will give you growth and a healthy bottom line.

35

BRANDING YOUR COMPANY

WHEN I MEET with and talk with a CEO, I always like to ask him about his company's brand and brand identity. You'd be surprised at how many CEOs cannot answer my questions. It's something they've thought about on a very cursory level, but usually without much careful thought and prayer. They get so caught up in the "daily grind" and forget the importance of carving out a brand identity in the marketplace. This is something we did very early on at my company, and it's paid off handsomely over the years.

Why is it important to create and build a brand identity? It's not enough to say, for example, you sell tires. And it's also not enough to simply choose a logo and color scheme. A true brand identity gives your business a personality. There's a huge amount of competition today, so businesses need to go the extra mile of ensuring they stand out in the crowd. To do this, you should invest in creating a strong brand that will get and keep people's attention. With the right branding, you have the chance to get some control over how people perceive your business. Customers have a lot to choose from, and without a brand identity, your company will look very much like all the others.

A brand identity is how you'll look different. It's how your customers and potential customers can tell the difference, apart from such things as price. You don't just want customers who recognize your brand and use your business once—you want to create customers who continue to come back. So with good branding, you can give your brand a more human side, which your customers can relate to more than a company that's strictly all business.

In many ways, you can appeal to people's emotions through branding and make them feel more connected to your company. Branding allows you to build personal relationships with your audience, which can eventually turn them into loyal customers. You can create a brand that people actually care about and put yourself ahead of businesses that aren't using this to their advantage. Let me offer an example of a company we are all familiar with, Apple.

When Steve Jobs returned to Apple in 1997, the tech company he co-founded more than two decades earlier was on the brink of failure. During the final quarter of 1996, Apple's sales plummeted by 30 percent, and Microsoft had become the dominant computer company in the market. Moving forward, Jobs's strategy was to recreate Apple and its product line. He literally tore the company apart, single-handedly destroyed Apple's silo units, and forced the entire company to work together as a single and cohesive unit—all under the same brand identity. Before Jobs's return, Apple had not developed a true brand. He asked himself and the entire Apple team to answer four questions about the company and its products:

- Who are we? (Brand identity)

- What are we? (Brand meaning)

- How does the customer feel about us? (Brand response)

- What about you and me? (Brand relationship)

At first glance, these probably seem simple, and if I were to ask you these questions, you might flippantly offer up some answers. But I cannot emphasize enough how important it is to thoroughly think and pray about these in terms of you and your company. For Steve Jobs and Apple, they answered "Who are we?" with these three words: simple, unique, and innovators. Many years after they answered this question, it's still very clear in all of our minds that they are indeed simple, unique, and innovators. They set their course and stayed focused on their brand identity. It worked! So who are you? What three words best describe your story?

"What are we?" is a bit harder to answer. For Apple, they wanted to be "a solution for life, all about communication, and a profitable company." Indeed they are a profitable company. I would argue one of the reasons they are profitable is because they set out to be profitable. It was a part of their branding. So what are you? Not who, but what? Try to describe what you desire to be as a company in words that are direct and specific.

Then ask yourself, "How does the customer feel about us?" Apple's customers, by design, feel excited, good, and sacrificial. That's right, sacrificial. They literally want their customers to spend a fortune with Apple. They want customers to feel so excited, they're willing to spend a premium for their products. So as you can see, this was not an accident for Apple. This was a part of their brand identity. How do you want your customers to feel about you? In other words, what response do you want your customers to give you when doing business with you?

Finally, what about you and me? What kind of relationships do you want to have with your customers? Steve Jobs wanted his customer relationships to involve loyalty, trustworthiness, and love. Yes, love! I think it's incredible that Apple used the word "love" in its branding. Many years later, it's still true. Apple customers love Apple. How would you best describe the kind of relationships you want with your customers? Think long and hard about it, because once you establish it, chances are it will come true, just as it did for Apple.

The bottom line is that people don't tend to have relationships with products and services; their loyalty and commitment is to the brand.

If no branding is applied, your customers will just as easily buy from someone else who sells a similar product or brand. It's time to stand out from the crowd, be different, and be someone your customers recognize in a personal way.

36

FEED YOUR SHEEP!

SUCCESSFUL CEOS AND business owners learn that it costs more money to attract a new customer than to keep an existing one. Rather than working overtime to find a new customer, you'll probably do better to keep the customers you have, to keep them happy, and to sell them more of your products and services. Great customer service even sometimes results in your customers becoming your greatest advocates, which saves you even more marketing dollars.

There are also clear biblical commands to treat your customers as you would treat yourself. Since every customer is made in God's image, communication should reflect that dignity. So with our customers, we practice empathy, we work hard to communicate clearly, we listen with grace, and we respond with respect. Even when we err and a customer becomes irate, the New Testament reiterates the need to be "quick to hear, slow to speak and slow to anger" (James 1:19). Our team has learned to strive to "walk the talk" with our customers, and we've become famous for our biblical response to customer service issues.

But it's not enough to simply *assume* that your customers are happy. Sometimes customers don't tell you they aren't happy. They bail out, and before you know it, you've lost your customer to a competitor. Other times, a team member may not fully inform you or his manager that a customer is unhappy. Again, you've lost a customer. So how can you know if your customers are happy? Is there a guaranteed way to know?

Information gathered from customer service surveys will tell you—specifically, a Net Promoter Score (NPS), which is the gold standard of customer experience metrics. We've learned to rely on the NPS, and it's transformed how we measure our customers' experience. By using the NPS to collect feedback, we learn what makes our customers happy and what makes them unhappy.

Information gathered helps us validate decisions and demonstrates to our customers that we're sincerely interested in serving their needs. We discover who's satisfied and who's dissatisfied, and why.

The beauty of the NPS is that it's brief, simple, easy to ask, and easy to answer. It measures customer perception based on one simple question, and it literally takes thirty seconds to answer. In this way, our customers almost always respond. Customer responses are also easy for our team to analyze, as results are reduced to three metrics:

- **The detractor**: These are your dissatisfied customers, the angry ones who have an issue with your product, your service, or your team. Respond to them speedily and get to the bottom of their discontent. Work hard to win them back.

- **The mutual/passive**: They're generally happy but not enough to become raving fans, mostly unenthusiastic customers who are vulnerable to competitive offerings. They are easier to win back with better communication.

- **The loyalist/promoter**: They love you! Find ways to reward them and build partnerships so they'll refer other customers to you. Consider gifts and discounts, and find ways to celebrate their success.

The beauty of the NPS is that it reduces complex issues to simple solutions. You can measure almost anything using an NPS score. Also consider implementing it into your sales and marketing because it can be compared to industry benchmarks to see how you measure up to your competitors. It can help you better understand your target market and learn how they respond to your sales offerings.

Remember the goal is to gain loyal customers who become brand evangelists instead of consumers.

37

BE A STRATEGIC PLANNER

I've always said that you cannot manage what you don't measure and monitor. Every single CEO I talk to agrees with me, yet few will follow through with consistent and systematic strategic planning. In fact, according to the *Harvard Business Review*,[5] 50 percent of executive leadership spends no time at all working on a strategic planning process. Is that you?

Maybe you don't do strategic planning because you don't understand it. Simply put, strategic planning is an organizational management activity that is used to set your priorities, to focus your resources, to strengthen your operations, and to ensure that team members and other stakeholders are all working toward common goals. It's a disciplined effort, not just casual conversation, and it should result in an actual document that will shape and guide what your organization is, who it serves, what it does, and why it does it, with a concentrated focus on the future.

Strategic planning is a year-long process. It never ends for us, but we set aside dedicated time at the end of the year to take a deep dive. Our management team meets together to review, assess, and decide what's working and what's not. Then we refocus our efforts in an intentional and strategic way. While there are many different frameworks and methodologies for strategic planning and management, and no absolute rules regarding the right framework, I'll share with you what works for our organization.

We focus our strategic planning on five distinct areas. But our overarching theme always surrounds what the Lord is telling us. We begin and end every strategic planning review with prayer, thanking God for what He's done and asking for His wisdom as we peer into the future. This reminds us that Jesus is our CEO! Also, we believe God wants His people to be disciplined and orderly, not haphazard, for maximum kingdom impact. Here are the five areas we like to focus on. You may want to custom tailor your own efforts, but consider including all of these areas:

- **Ministry impact.** We don't leave this to chance. We purposefully review how our organization is impacting the world for the Gospel, including our giving and charitable contributions. But we also look at how we are impacting souls for the Gospel and ministering as individuals and as a group.

- **Operational management.** We ask management to assess our operations, which includes activities that our business engages in on a daily basis to increase the value of the enterprise and earn a profit. Operations means different things for different businesses, but try to think about it as everything involved in producing and fulfilling your products and services.

- **Organizational development.** Your people are your most valuable asset, so take time to carefully look at how you are recruiting, hiring, training, supporting, and managing your people. This area is often overlooked, but we place high value on also making this area strategic and not haphazard. Human resources can make or break your organization, so plan for it.

- **Financial management**. By "financial management," I don't mean sales. I mean how we are accounting for each and every dollar that comes in and goes out of the company. We look at such areas as cost control, financial accountability, accounts receivables and payables, and the budgeting process. For this area, it's a good opportunity for your financial team to better collaborate with the rest of your company.

- **Revenue generation**. This is, of course, a very important area. We take time as a team to review what products are selling, what products are not selling, and why. We involve not just our sales and marketing team in this discussion, but also the entire management team. I like to get a macro view of the sale process to better understand and refocus our revenue strategy. You'd be surprised what you sometimes learn about sales from your non-sales team.

However you pursue strategic planning in your organization, the end result should be a well-thought-out document that everyone feels a part of, everyone will buy into, and everyone will revisit during the year. This helps us avoid unexpected crises and the feeling that we spend most of our time putting out fires. It provides clarity and reminds us that there can be a semblance of control and order as we each do our work. But don't forget, God is in control, not you!

38

ORGANIC VS. INVESTED

Most CEOs I talk to are looking for more money, more capital, more investors, or more debt to somehow transform their businesses into something bigger and better. Rather than looking inward, they look outward. They believe their magic wand is more funding, and they spend a lot of time thinking about and talking to others about it. "If only I could find an investor," one CEO told me. "I'm going to start crowdfunding," said another, "and then I'll have enough money to grow." To someone laboring in a cash-strapped startup, money often seems to be the end-game. Will all your problems go away if you had more money? Maybe. Maybe not. It's certainly not guaranteed, and I've seen many businesses literally end up in a worse predicament.

There are some things that definitely come with other people's money. They're new and different problems. Before you decide that it's absolutely necessary to take outside investment, explore all the possible ways you can partner, outsource, affiliate, collaborate, or otherwise work on your business. This might be hard to hear, but before you take another dime or dollar, you need to spend more time working on and in your business. If you think you have problems now, imagine how much worse your problems will be when your business is STILL not working AND you have obligations to investors or debtors. Then you'll really be in a bad position.

My advice, and this is based on my own experiences, is to do everything in your power to grow your company organically before you look for more funding. Dig deep and discover what's broken in your business and why. Ask yourself, "What about my business is not exceptional?" "Why aren't more customers calling?" "What is lacking in my customer experience?" "What about my product?" "Why isn't it working for more customers, and why aren't they raving about it online?"

I believe that part or possibly the entire problem is that you aren't paying attention to organic growth. It's not magic and it's hard work, but it pays off more than any investor or loan you'll ever find.

We live in an era when customers post in a very public way what they like or dislike about the products and services they purchase. Did you know that 90 percent of buyers are more likely to convert after reading reviews? This statistic alone makes one thing clear: If your business isn't prioritizing high-quality review generation, you could be losing out on 90 percent of your customers, value-adding relationships, and recurring revenue. Needless to say, product and service reviews are a big deal. Reading, evaluating, and applying peer insights has become a necessity before purchasing a solution, and online reputation holds more value now than ever before.

So spend time on ramping up on how you sell to and support your customers. Make it work with what you have, and then spend more time working out an organic growth plan rather than on taking someone else's money.

The challenge of landing that capital to grow a company can be exhilarating. But as exciting as the money search may be, it can be dangerous. The lure of fast money leads founders to grossly underestimate the time, effort, and creative energy it takes to get more cash in the bank.

This is perhaps the least appreciated aspect of raising money. In emerging companies, during the fundraising cycle, owners commonly devote more time in fundraising than in running their business. I've seen entrepreneurs drop nearly everything else they were working on to find potential money sources and tell their story. The process is stressful and can drag on for months or even years, all while their business is failing. The emotional and physical drain leaves little energy for running the business, and cash is flowing out rather than in. It's a surefire way to go bankrupt.

If you focus your time and energy on figuring out what will make your business work now, while it's still small, you'll eventually not need outside investor funding. You won't need debt, or at least not as much of it. An organic growth plan, if successful, will be extraordinarily more beneficial in the long run. Be a good steward of what you have, and God will see you through!

39

THE SECRET TO CASH FLOW

TOO MANY CEOS focus more on their profit and loss statement than on their balance sheet. In fact, sometimes it's all they focus on. They concentrate on making sure they are making more money than they are spending, which is of course important. It's all about being profitable, right? But at the end of the day, they often have very little cash in the bank, which causes all sorts of internal challenges, and it confuses them because they know they are profitable. The problem isn't that they are losing money. The problem is that they can't keep up on a daily basis with cash flow.

This is how I learned to think about it.

A profit and loss (or income) statement lists your sales and expenses. It tells you how much profit you're making or how much you're losing. This is a very important barometer of your business's health. It shows you the efficiency and effectiveness of both your sales and expenses. If your profit and loss statement shows a consistent loss, you're in trouble.

A balance sheet is a statement of your business's assets, liabilities, and equity (what you own in the business) as of any given date. This is also an important barometer, and in some ways it's a more important way to measure your company's health. If your balance sheet rarely shows any cash, you're going to get into trouble—cash flow trouble.

Cash flow is the amount of cash and cash equivalents (such as securities) that your business generates or spends over a set time period. Cash flow differs from profit, which is why and how it's reflected on a balance sheet. Cash flow refers to the money that flows in and out of your business. Profit is the money you have after deducting your business expenses from overall revenue. You need to generate enough cash from your business activities so you can meet your expenses and have enough left over to grow the business. While a company can temporarily fudge its earnings, you can't fake cash flow. You either have cash or you don't. And if you don't, everyone will know about it!

I find that cash flow challenges cause more stress and anxiety on CEOs than just about anything. Meeting payroll and paying vendors can become all-consuming tasks and can literally sink a company. There are many ways to improve your cash flow, but I discovered three key components that helped us survive and take control of our balance sheet.

First, negotiate terms with your vendors. Don't accept that your vendors will always demand to be paid on short terms. You might be surprised at how some vendors may extend your terms from weeks to even months later than originally requested from you. If you're able to extend your payment terms even a few weeks out, it will significantly improve your cash standing.

Second, do the same with your customers. While you want to be realistic, reasonable, and always respectful with your customers, you may also be surprised at how willing some may be to pay you sooner than later. Some customers may be willing to pay you immediately without any terms. Sometimes, if you offer them a small benefit (cost savings), it will be worth it to get your cash now.

Finally, build a solid accounts receivable process. This is one area that needs careful and constant attention. Ask your accounting team to provide you with accurate and updated A/R aging reports, which will track and measure the payment status of all your customers. Be proactive in your invoicing and collection efforts, making sure all parties are on the same page regarding payment deadlines, amounts owed, and payment methods. If you have past-due receivables, ask your accounting team to move fast. Sometimes it helps to offer a small discount to get your receivables up to date.

These are simple, actionable steps that any CEO can implement immediately. If you're stressed out about your business, despite it being profitable, I predict you have a cash flow problem. Remember that cash is king. Also remember that Jesus is THE King of your business. Ask Him to help you build a strong balance sheet!

40

PAID MARKETING

MOST CEOS LOOK to their marketing department to drive exposure and ultimately increase sales. They look to their customer service department to support those who've already made a purchase. So marketing is pre-sale and customer service is post-sale. This is the wrong way to look at and think about marketing and customer service.

Before I dive in, let me share a story about one of the most recognized and reputable brands in the hotel industry, Ritz-Carlton. "The Ritz" is famous for its cigar bars. A hotel guest, after checking in, requested a specific brand of cigar. The hotel, of course, delivered the cigar to his room. Later, the traveler checked in to a Ritz hotel in another location. Upon entering his room, he noticed the same cigar brand sitting on his desk, waiting for him.

You might think, "That's great customer service." Indeed it is. But it's even better marketing. Undoubtedly, this man has become a walking and talking advertisement for the Ritz-Carlton brand. He even made it into my book!

Marketing is important and also expensive. But the best marketing campaign you'll ever create is transforming your customers into raving fans. Organic marketing is the best, cheapest, and most effective kind of marketing. You achieve that through great customer service. You'll always need marketing. No business can thrive without it. But when you create customers that fall in love with your product or service, and how you deliver it, the end result will be free marketing.

We can look to Jesus and His ministry for an example of how to take care of your customers. Jesus loved people, and He spent a great deal of time and effort showing it. He even washed their feet. I think we forget about how Jesus not only loved on people, but He also approached them with great detail. He considered what was really important to people and He showed it, even if that meant washing feet.

Is this how you look at and manage your customer service? Do you think about and execute it as support or as marketing? The world's best and biggest brands build their customer experience in a way that transforms their customers into effective organic marketing. They understand that great customer service is in the detail.

Great customer service means following best practices such as valuing customers' time, having a pleasant attitude, and providing knowledgeable and resourceful resources, but that you also go a step further to exceed—rather than just meet—expectations. You can't do this unless you pay attention to the details.

What does this mean? At my company, we've built the customer service experience into the entire company, from top to bottom. Here are a few of the most important things we've done to create raving fans, and you can, too.

Know your product

Your job is to help your customers get the most out of their purchases and feel that they are getting true value. Make sure your team members are product experts so they can amaze your customers with their knowledge. Your customers will respect your team more if they believe they've taken the time to truly understand what they are selling. It will keep them coming back.

Maintain a positive attitude

Attitude is everything, and a positive attitude goes a long way in providing excellent customer service. Since most customer interactions are not face-to-face these days, your attitude should be reflected in your language and tone of voice. Just as Chick-fil-A does so well, we also say "My pleasure" instead of just "Thank you." Want smiling customers? Smile at them first!

Respond quickly

Resolving customer queries as quickly as possible is a cornerstone of good customer service. Speed should be of the essence—especially for smaller issues that don't take much time to solve. Customers don't want to languish in a ticket queue, but they'll spend as much time as it takes to resolve their issues. You should, too.

Try to personalize your service

Customers want to feel like more than a ticket number. They want to interact with a person—not a company. They get angry when they're not being treated like an individual person, receiving boilerplate responses. Do you know not only your customers' names, but also their birthdates? How about their interests or hobbies? It's obviously not possible to do this for everyone, but going off script with a detailed personal touch will show them you care.

Keep your word

If you promise something, making sure you deliver on it is common-sense customer service. Don't let your customers down. Keeping your word is about respect and trust. If you break your word, offer something to make up for it. If your customer's delivery goes awry, offer to replace it and refund his money for his trouble. You might lose some money in the short term, but you'll gain a loyal custome

41

HOW TO BE FOOD-CENTRIC

AVE YOU EVER wondered why food was so central to Jesus' ministry? So much of what we learn about Jesus occurred during meals, from the wedding feast where Jesus turned the water into wine, to Zacchaeus asking Jesus to dinner, to Jesus feeding five thousand people with five small barley loaves and two small fish, to the Last Supper and when Jesus appeared to His disciples at breakfast near the Sea. Jesus said to us, "I am the bread of life; he who comes to Me will not hunger, and he who believes in Me will never thirst" (John 6:35). He also broke bread it and gave it to His disciples saying, "This is My body which is given for you; do this in remembrance of Me" (Luke 22:19). I bet you didn't realize how often Jesus's teaching and miracles surrounded food and even wine.

How is it important to you as a CEO and business leader that Jesus's ministry surrounded food? Food brings us together in a special and unique way. The sharing of food has brought people together since the beginning of time. It's how we make friends, nurture our relationships, celebrate milestones, and feel gratitude for life. Think about your favorite foods. Perhaps it's your dad's barbeque ribs or your wife's secret-recipe brownies. Maybe it's that steak you ate on an important and successful business trip to

Chicago or the one-of-a-kind pizza you ate with your wife in New York City when you proposed to her. Chances are, your favorite food is connected to someone or somewhere because food is the one thing that never fails to bring people together. The emotions that come from sharing food are universal, and it conquers all, from language barriers to cultural differences.

When we started our company in 2004, we recognized that one way we could bond our team together in a unique, long-lasting, and memorable way was through food. We learned this from reading our Bibles and simply from our own experiences. So we set our course to provide the entire staff with a free two-hour lunch each Friday. It wasn't cheap, and it wasn't always easy, but I can honestly say it's been one of the best things we ever did. Years later, a staff member will remind me of a story that surrounded one of our Friday meals. It became a tradition that the team looks forward to each and every week. It builds trust among team members, and it simply makes it more fun to come to work, especially on a Friday, after a long week on the job.

But we don't stop there. We find all sorts of opportunities to use food as a way to build rapport and relationships with our team. When we have celebrations in the workplace, for individual staff members or for the entire team when we've reached a goal, they always include food. Whether it's a cake, cookies, donuts, or a full-course meal, we celebrate with food. The team loves the breaks, and a well-fed staff member is a productive staff member! We even use Uber Eats to deliver food to the homes of staff members when remote work is required.

Remember that within days of leaving bondage in Egypt and heading toward the land God had promised His people, they began to grumble and pine for the comforts of their old life. They wanted food! So the Lord caused bitter water to become sweet and even led them to an oasis to camp during the journey. He fed them by providing meat via large flocks of quail that flew into their camp each evening and miraculous dew in the mornings that turned into flakes of sweet bread (manna) for them to eat. God knows the importance of food, as He created it for us. So as a CEO, be like Moses, be like Jesus, and feed your people!

42

INVESTORS VS. NO INVESTORS

WHEN I CONSULT with or counsel other CEOs, they frequently ask me how they can raise money to achieve their growth goals. They are often looking for investment dollars in the form of equity or debt, more cash or capital, a bank loan, or other forms of outside funding. Whether they are seeking money from one single investor or crowdfunding from a multitude of investors, they are squarely focused on the notion that if they could access more cash, they could grow their company faster and more profitably.

My advice, which is sometimes unpopular among the CEOs I know, is based in part on how we've built our company. Aside from $50,000 in seed funds to launch, we've never raised money in the form of equity or debt investments. Instead, we've focused on delivering high-quality products and services. We've achieved steady, organic growth based on strong leadership, not somebody else's money. Certainly there have been times we've flirted with the idea of finding outside funding, but we've held fast to the idea that natural growth is a better way to grow a company. Let me explain.

Starting and running a company is hard work. It takes passion, endurance, and a lot of prayer.

All the personal sacrifices and long hours are supposed to be rewarded when your startup becomes a profitable company. If you don't have investors, you are fully rewarded for your work. Do you really want to share it with someone else? In our case, we donate 50 percent of our company's profits to charitable causes. If we had investors, we'd have to share the funds we give away to our investor(s). That would be somewhat discouraging.

In addition to sharing profit, investors can take away some of your control. In some instances, investors get equity in your company in exchange for their investment. With this equity, they may have a say in what happens with the company. Many entrepreneurs start new businesses because they want freedom and independence, but if they take on an investor, they may lose that. Imagine someone else trying to tell you what to do, someone who doesn't even understand your business. Imagine trying to persuade an investor otherwise, particularly if your investor is not a believer in Christ. This would be a major distraction.

While it's tempting to be the recipient of a large check, remember that bigger is not necessarily better. Consider this: Owning 100 percent of a company worth $10 million is more lucrative than owning 1 percent of a company worth $100 million! Taking too much money prematurely, while giving part of your company away, can literally stifle growth as you might scale too quickly. Premature scaling has caused many startups to fail.

Finally, I believe you learn so much from doing it yourself rather than skipping the learning phase. Digging in and learning the ins and outs of your product or service will equip you to make better business decisions. You will learn your core competencies, better evaluate opportunities, and pivot when the right opportunities present themselves. You can also know when the wrong opportunities come along and avoid them. Also, when you don't have cash to pay someone to help you with your business, you have to find other ways of achieving your goals. You have to get creative. In my experience, this creativity can open doors. It makes you more agile, and it makes you smarter. Necessity is an excellent teacher.

The Bible is clear about taking on debt. Any form of investment you take is a form of debt, as eventually it has to be paid back. Debt is a form of slavery, it prevents rest and increased anxiety, it compromises your ability to be agile and flexible, and it can literally become a form of greed. "For the Lord your God will bless you, as he promised you, and you shall lend to many nations, but you shall not borrow, and you shall rule over many nations, but they shall not rule over you" (Deuteronomy 15:6).

There are instances where investment, even some debt, makes prudent sense. But in most cases, a CEO would be wise to seriously consider organic growth rather than trying to speed a company to growth and profits.

43

MAKE CRM A PRIORITY

HAVE YOU EVER wondered why Jesus chose only twelve disciples? He could have asked dozens of people to His inner circle of friends and followers, even hundreds. It would seem to be a better idea to have more dedicated followers rather than less. But He recruited only twelve people to be with Him as He traveled and ministered. That's not very many people.

As I pondered this in a personal and spiritual way, I was also working behind the scenes at my company to find more effective ways to reach out to and respond to our customers. I was frustrated that we seemed to be losing touch with too many of them, even dropping the ball on occasion. When I investigated a bit further with my sales and customer support team, I discovered that they lacked an efficient and effective means of organizing their customers. They told me that without a good system and process, they can keep track of and manage only about ten to twelve customers.

Did you get that? They could manage only a very small number, about ten to twelve. This was a light-bulb moment for me! I always look to the Bible for guidance, and I realized that even Jesus understood that you can manage only a limited number of people without losing touch. Jesus invested His time and energy into a group of people that He could impact. My business problem was that I was asking my team members to manage too many customers at once. They were burdened and overwhelmed. This was my introduction to Customer Relationship Management (CRM) software. Through CRM, I could help my team do what Jesus did: build strong relationships with a small number of people.

What is a CRM system? It's a customer-centric platform that connects your different departments, from marketing to sales to customer service, and organizes their notes, activities, and metrics. Each user has direct access to the real-time client data he needs about each customer. It helps you store customer and prospect contact information, identify sales opportunities, record service issues, and even manage marketing campaigns. This not only allows for more efficient coordination across teams and departments, but it also makes it possible to provide their customers with something extraordinary: personalized, one-to-one customer journeys. You can build relationships with hundreds, even thousands, that look and feel personal, just as if you were working with only twelve people.

My sales and customer support staff reported almost instant benefits, and over time, our sales steadily increased as we could better manage our customer relationships. Customers reported feeling more relevant and appropriate communication from us, and as a result, they purchased more of our products. In other words, they could feel the love!

When we started to deploy CRM in our organization, I also discovered many other benefits that helped me be a better CEO, including:

- Trustworthy reporting information, allowing me to better track our progress.

- Real-time dashboards that visually showcase our customer relationships.

- Improved communication with my own team members, particularly when someone needs help.

- Simplified collaboration between sales and marketing. Finally, marketing can see what's working!

- Better goal-setting, as we have a more realistic view of leads and conversions.

- More upselling and cross-selling opportunities.

- Reduce wasted time on prospects that probably won't ever become customers.

Remember in His early months of ministry in Israel, Jesus attracted great multitudes to hear His messages, receive His miraculous healings, and eat the bread He offered. But the Jewish leaders rejected Him and claimed that His power came from Satan, yet the people—for the most part—flocked after Him. But it appears that His ministry didn't prosper until He asked twelve people to trust in Him completely and to submit to His authority as the "bread from heaven." Jesus began a six-month period of private instruction with the twelve, those He would prepare for the time of His ascension. This small group eventually took His teachings to the world and changed it. Don't underestimate the importance of how CRM software can help your team also change your company!

44

UPSELL AND CROSS-SELL

W HAT DOES JESUS have to do with sales and marketing? When you make Jesus your CEO, He will guide your business in every way, even including how you sell your products and services. I've learned to rely on God and His Word in all aspects of my business. Here's an example that can help you exponentially increase your revenue and profit.

Early on in my business, I didn't emphasize upselling and cross-selling. Once I identified a new customer, I simply sold him my product and I went on with my business. But I eventually learned that finding new customers is expensive. So I found ways to sell more products to my existing customers, which was more profitable than spending all my time and resources finding new ones. I also discovered that my existing customers appreciated it when I found new ways to solve their problems and save them money. It was a win-win! So this became a real focus, and it's benefited our company.

I do this in two distinct ways: upsell and cross-sell. Let me explain what I mean, and also how the Bible explains it. Remember, Jesus is your CEO!

Upselling is asking customers to purchase a comparable higher-end product than the one they first ask for, while cross-selling invites your customers to buy complimentary items that are related. Though used interchangeably, upselling and cross-selling both offer distinct benefits and provide value to your customers. They will increase your revenue without recurring and expensive marketing costs. Cross-selling and upselling are similar in that they both focus on providing additional value to your customers, and your job as a CEO is to understand what your customers value and then respond with upsell and cross-sell opportunities.

Upselling is the process of showing your customers how other versions, higher-end versions, of your products might better fulfill their needs. Companies that excel at upselling are effective at helping customers visualize the value they will get by ordering a higher-priced item. Don't be afraid to upsell. While your customers are looking for value, they are also looking for quality. Sometimes high quality means better value. So don't be bashful.

Cross-selling identifies products that satisfy additional needs that are unfulfilled by the original sale. For example, paperclips and staplers could be cross-sold to a customer purchasing paper for the office. Oftentimes, cross-selling points users to products they would have purchased anyway; by showing them at the right time, you ensure that they are buying them from you instead of from a competitor. Cross-selling is prevalent in every type of commerce, and if you're not doing it, you're missing out.

The Bible shows us examples of upselling and cross-selling. When Jesus walked the shores of the Sea of Galilee, he found a fisherman named Peter. He offered Peter the opportunity to become more than a fisherman: a "fisher of men." You could say that Jesus was cross-selling! He used words and metaphors Peter was familiar with, and He offered him the opportunity to fish for more than food, but for the "bread of life." Peter agreed and spent the rest of his life fishing for both biological and spiritual sustenance.

The Bible also shows us the importance of upselling. Everything Jesus said and did was an "upsell" because He called us to something greater. He showed His disciples how to live a different life, a better life, a life focused on His love and eternal life. Then He told them, "Very truly I tell you, whoever believes in me will do the works I have been doing, and they will do even GREATER THINGS than these, because I am going to the Father" (John 14:12). Jesus presents us with the world's greatest upsell opportunity: Believe in Him, and you will have eternal life!

As a CEO, your job is to grow your company. Upselling and cross-selling will increase your customer retention, increase the average order value and lifetime value of your customers, and show your customers that you care about them. Just as Jesus did, you want to give your customers the opportunity to get more value, solve more problems, and save. Never stop thinking of ways to give your customers something greater!

45

A BETTER PRICING STRATEGY

THIS GOES WITHOUT saying, but I'll say it because too many Christian CEOs still fail to understand it: Your pricing position will determine your Kingdom impact. When you price your products or services too low or too high, you're literally damaging your profit and loss statement to the extent that your company's value is losing ground. Eventually you'll lose your position in the marketplace and even lose your business entirely.

Most CEOs use pricing models that are externally focused. Rather than starting with their own story or brand, they start with someone else's. They assign pricing models either randomly, based on what they see around them, or they look specifically at their competitor's pricing and mimic it. They view it as an event rather than a process. In fact, in a recent survey of its members by the Professional Pricing Society,[6] 30 percent of respondents said they priced new products by simply mirroring their nearest competitors.

While it's not a bad thing to consider how similar products and services are priced, if that's the only consideration, chances are you're assigning less than prudent pricing. Other research suggests that a pricing process, rather than random or competitor-based, can increase your company's profitability from 25 to 75 percent. I don't know any CEOs who wouldn't want to see that!

I'm a strong proponent that your pricing ought to be internally developed and based on your company's story, brand, and position. Story-based pricing accounts for how you want to be perceived in the market. It accounts for the values that are built in to your company and how you want customers to think about you. The most common mistake CEOs make when pricing is to ignore their own story.

Here's what I mean. Think about Walmart; now think about Neiman Marcus. Think about McDonald's; now think about Ruth's Chris Steak House. You get the idea. Different company values, different stories, different pricing. If you decide to take a premium price position, you can expect to attract customers with more expendable income. So your company's story must match "premium." You can't look like WalMart and try to sell like Neiman Marcus. It doesn't match. If you decide to take a value price position, but you look and feel upscale, it doesn't match. Imagine walking into Walmart and it looks like Neiman Marcus!

Think about it this way: Your brand is your promise to your customers. It's what they expect from you when they do business with you. Your prices are just as important to brand equity as other differentiators because price conveys a quality message, and therefore it influences the conceptual place your company takes in your target customer's mind. What I believe is that when a CEO under-prices or over-prices, the customers are confused because they don't understand who you are as a company.

The Bible doesn't specifically address pricing models. However, if you want your company to reflect the heart of God, one of your jobs as a CEO is to carefully and prayerfully define who you are as a company. Pricing is an important way to do that. So rather than pricing yourself randomly or based on your competition, start with who you are and your desired position in the marketplace.

46

PARTNERS, NOT VENDORS

W E LOOK AT vendor relationships in a different way than do many organizations. We view a vendor as an ally more than someone who just sells us products. Sometimes there's a fine line between vendor and partner, but we lean toward being partners rather than being in an adversarial relationship, and it's helped our business. It's also become a way to minister the Gospel. Let me explain.

You and your entire team are ambassadors of the Gospel. This means every interaction you have is an opportunity to give testimony to Jesus, including with your vendors. Every conversation, every negotiation with your vendors, is an opportunity to give testimony to the Lord. The Bible says, "You are a letter from Christ ... written not with ink but with the Spirit of the Living God, not on tablets of stone but on tablets of human hearts" (2 Corinthians 3:3). Your vendors and the people who work for your vendors are watching you as you navigate each day. They know you are a believer in Jesus, they see how you respond to them, and it speaks loudly. Even if you never say a word or write a note, you are sharing your testimony by what you do and the way you talk and act. When you act in a way that shows you are a loving and caring person, your vendors are aware.

But there's another reason, a business reason, to building relationships with your vendors that are built on trust and respect. John Maxwell once said, "Teamwork makes the dream work, but the vision becomes a nightmare when the leader has a big dream and a bad team." This also applies well when looking at your organization's supply chain, which includes your vendors. Establishing and maintaining solid vendor relationships is crucial to your customer service, your cost efficiency, the quality of your products, and even future market development. Your vendors are your allies in business, and they can play a crucial role in the success or failure of your organization. If things go bad with your vendors, your business is in trouble!

What does this mean, in terms of your business relationship with your vendors? As a CEO, you should work to nurture your vendor relationships in the same way you nurture your customers. Both relationships are *equally* important. Having a great relationship with a supplier who has a vested interest in your business can prove to be beneficial.

What does this mean in a strategic and tactical way?

Most companies try to take advantage of their vendors in terms of their costs and terms. They are constantly looking for the best price and the longest terms. They try to "milk" the relationship for every single penny, and the relationships look and feel antagonistic. Some CEOs are constantly dumping one vendor for another, always skipping around looking for the best "deal." I can tell you that if you do this, the long-term consequences for your business are going to be negative.

We take a different view. First, we look at our vendor relationships as an opportunity to spread the Gospel. But we also place high value on the relationships from a revenue and profit perspective. We don't demand "cheap" from our vendors. We look for a good price, of course, but we don't regularly menace them with demands for a better price and longer terms. Once a year, we review our vendor relationships, and if appropriate, we will negotiate better terms. But once we do that, we stick to our word and work hard to build a relationship built on respect and trust. In this way, our vendors fight for us. They view us as partners, and they look for ways to help our business grow and to become more profitable. And if there are issues with their supply chain, we're the first to know. This high level of collaboration leads to the distinction between barebones offering and service to handcrafted solutions that are win-win.

It's also a win-win for Jesus!

47

THE PURSUIT OF PROFIT/MONEY

THERE WAS A time when I looked at my company's profit and loss statement daily. I would take a deep dive into the itemized details and analyze both the top line and bottom line revenue and profits. I'd ask questions of my staff about it and ask for constant updates. I'd even lose sleep over it. I was, as you can imagine, consumed by the money coming in and going out of my business. Frankly, I did not think this was a sinful thing to do. I knew that pursuing money was dangerous and that the love of money is the root of all evil. But I didn't view it as "loving" money. I viewed it as being concerned about money and the health of the company. I eventually realized, however, that being consumed with money is the same thing as loving money. The Lord convicted me and I changed my ways.

Economist John Kenneth Galbraith once observed, "Money is a singular thing. It ranks with love as man's greatest source of joy—and with death as his greatest source of anxiety." Are you, as a CEO and business owner, consumed with money? Do you constantly worry about it, look at it, ask questions about it, have dreams and nightmares about it? If so, I encourage you in the Lord to do what I did and change how you think about money. You certainly should change how *often* you think about it.

Don't think you are alone. Every single CEO that I've ever known has been consumed by money, at least at one time. Most of us are prone to worrying about money, but business owners more so. It's important to understand, however, that Jesus wants all His followers to be free from worries about money—business owners included! Don't think that just because you own a business and are responsible for other people's income that you're excluded from the words of Jesus. Remember, after Jesus was speaking to the crowd about the dangers of greed and living for this world without a view to eternity (Luke 12), He spoke to His disciples (his leaders), who perhaps felt anxious about whether they would have enough to live on. He showed them that anxiety is diametrically opposed to trusting in God, who lovingly cares for His own. He also showed that to go to the other extreme and pursue riches is at odds with seeking God's kingdom.

Jesus tells us to solve our worries about money, we must simply trust in the God who cares for us (Luke 12:22–28). This is far from blind optimism because it is based solidly on the nature and character of God and His many promises to us. And if you don't trust God when it comes to your company's finances, it will cut a dark and deep channel into which all your other thoughts are drained.

Here's what I did when I realized that I was consumed by money:

I stopped looking at money, and instead I looked at my company apart from money. Instead of being consumed with my financial statements, I became consumed with everything else inside my company, such as my people, our processes, and my customers and vendors. I walked "the floor" instead of sitting at my desk staring at my computer. I became engaged with my company. Guess what happened? My financial statements started to look even better when I looked at them!

I also stopped thinking about how to spend my money. If you find yourself spending more time deciding what to purchase next—be it a car, a house, or a cruise vacation—then, my friend, you're consumed with money. You're on the verge of making decisions that will eventually destroy your company. Your mission is *not* to make money, right? You need to put your mission statement on your desk and spend more time thinking about how to achieve your mission rather than how to spend your money.

"The purpose of business isn't making money," wrote Hubert Joly, the former CEO of Best Buy. "Making money is imperative, but it's not the purpose of business. Profit is like the temperature of a patient, the symptom of an underlying condition. Focusing on the symptom alone can be dangerous." Amen! Focus on Jesus and His will for you and your company, and get into the trenches with your team. Learn and understand your business from the ground up, and let God worry about the money!

48

WALKING THE FLOOR

BEING A CEO is a heavy responsibility. It's the CEO's responsibility to figure out how all the pieces fit together, to implement a plan and execute it, and to oversee the operation of the business. Staff members and vendors need to be paid, products need to be shipped, and the IRS needs its money too! The responsibility is all-encompassing and constant. There are times when you would like not to be responsible, even just for a short moment. But you are always responsible.

Being a CEO might be the loneliest job on the planet, yet despite the alone-ness of the job, CEOs often retreat into the "safety" of the office, avoiding staff. Sitting in front of the computer all day long feels safer than communicating in-person with your team. It's a common problem with CEOs and business leaders, and it has a detrimental effect on your company. When you spend too much time in the enclave of your office, you are literally hurting yourself and your team.

A recent study outlined in *Harvard Business Review*[7] uncovered how key executives handle their time to remain productive and efficient. The researchers, Michael E. Porter and Nitin Nohria, tracked CEOs over a three-month period, and they found the average CEO spends 6 percent of their time with rank-and-file staff. The same study also revealed that CEOs spend 28 percent of their time alone. It is shocking to find that they are alone for over one-fourth of their work time.

I noticed the same pattern begin to emerge in me when I started my own business. But when my company started to grow, I quickly realized how important it was to "walk the floor." It's not always an easy thing to do, and the natural or default setting is to walk into the office and close the door. But I found when I did that, soon I was closed off to my own team—and to my own company. Before I explain, I want to point to the kind of leader Jesus was.

The Bible clearly portrays Jesus as what we call a "people person." In fact, Jesus spent so much time with people that His disciples actually asked him to stop. In Matthew 14:15, they said to Jesus, "Tell the multitudes to go away!" Jesus refused. Time after time, Jesus was found spending a great deal of time with people, to the point of exhaustion. But He understood the importance of personal relationships.

As CEOs, we should look to Jesus when we go to the office. We should not do what the disciples asked Jesus to do. On the contrary, spend as much time with your team as you can possibly carve out. When you walk into your office and close the door, you're closing the door to opportunities to grow your company. Keep your door open and walk the floor. When you do, you'll also feel less alone when staff members feel that they confide in you. They truly do want to help you if you give them the change. I've discovered the more time I spend with my team, it helps in four distinct areas:

- **It builds relationships.** When you take time out of your schedule for your team members, it shows that they are important and that you care. When they know you care, you will gain their trust, respect, and support. These are the building blocks for the development of strong relationships. And, it is through relationships that you will have the greatest impact as their leader.

- **They will feel valued.** Your time is one of the most valuable gifts you have to offer. When you make time for your team members, they feel appreciated. When team members feel valued, they become loyal advocates for you as a leader and for the organization. They will want to champion both you and the company.

- **They become more engaged.** Your interest in your team members will make them feel important, which results in more communication and engagement. Engaged team members tackle challenges head on. They will also want to learn new skills, take better care of your customers, and frankly, work harder.

- **It keeps you in the loop.** You will find no better opportunity for open communication than when you are spending time, face-to-face, with your team members. You get a better sense of who they are, and they get a sense of who you are. You might just be amazed at how out of the loop you have really been once team members start opening up and sharing with you.

Don't be one of the 6 percent of CEOs who avoids their own staff. Be like Jesus. Get out with your people. Show them you care, and they will show you they care. Spread the love in the office!

49

GOLDEN RULE CUSTOMERS

IT SOMETIMES FRUSTRATES me, and I'm sure it does you as well, when you call to get customer support and you hear that recording: "Your call is very important to us. Please wait for the next available agent." And then they make their customers hold for so long that it would make most people wonder if their call really was important to them. Or when you finally do get through to customer service, they don't treat you like a person. They are impersonal and treat you like an account number. They answer the call with a stoic and less-than-enthusiastic tone of voice and follow with a series of impersonal questions about your account number, the last four digits of your social security number, and your mother's maiden name, and only then do they ask what they can help you with. It's enough to ruin any day!

Here's how we create a customer experience that won't ruin your day. As you read this book, you can probably tell that I don't separate my business life from my spiritual life. I approach my work day as I approach everything else in my life, with Jesus at the center. Jesus is my CEO. One area in particular, in my business, where I keep the Lord in charge is with my customers. I don't view customers as little revenue or profit generators. I treat them as people, and my entire team does the same.

The Bible gives us clear direction as to how we ought to treat people: "So in everything, do to others what you would have them do to you, for this sums up the Law and the Prophets" (Matthew 7:12). When Jesus gave us the "Golden Rule," He didn't mean before and after the workday. He meant all day long, every day, at work and at play. This means He commanded us to do to our customers what we have done for ourselves. That's a tall order! But it's a command, and as Bible-believing CEOs, we need to obey, right?

Recent research[8] actually points us in the same direction. It wasn't too long ago when every business owner claimed that the key to winning customers was in the quality or price of the product. But things have changed. Now, an even more important success factor has appeared. Customers no longer base their loyalty on price or product. Instead, they stay loyal with companies due to the *experience* they receive. If you can't learn how to treat them with care, respect, and even love, you'll lose them. Our modern, consumer-based economy has the upper hand when it comes to product selection. Customers today easily switch their loyalty to brands that fulfill their needs. But if the buying experience leaves a positive, lasting impression, both future sales and brand loyalty are guaranteed.

I believe that the art of treating a customer as a child of God is misunderstood by many Christian CEOs. This is the key to creating an experience customers will love. It's easy to think you're customer friendly when in fact you may not be. By substituting one term for the other—"customer" for "child of God"—you begin to see a customer as a person just like you. You wouldn't treat yourself like dirt, so why would you do the same to a customer? Be empathetic! The simple reframe that works is to see a customer as a human made by God, rather than just a customer.

Become obsessed with this point. Paint it all over your office and remind your team daily.

Empathy is everything when it comes to customers. The bottom line is this: Take the time to understand what the customer is thinking and feeling. When you learn to think and feel like a customer, a child of God, you unlock your own God-given human potential to fix his problems. Before you can build a brand that people love, you have to get to intimately know your audience: who they are, what motivates them, what makes them happy, what their challenges are, and why your brand is the solution they are seeking. When people visit your place of business, have your team members ask questions (and really listen) to build a better understanding of these prospects and how you can best serve them, as children of our living God!

50

TRY 360 REVIEWS

As the CEO of a Christ-centered organization, I always try to lead by example. Two of the areas I try to exemplify are honesty and accountability. While many companies develop highly politicized and bureaucratic cultures, we thrive on direct, honest feedback horizontally, not vertically. In other words, everyone is accountable to everyone, with Christ at the center.

One way we ensure that our team and individual team members feel empowered to be honest about their work is our 360 review process. Many organizations use the 360 review. If you don't, you should consider it. The 360 review is an employer-team member feedback opportunity that enables them to share feedback about each other. Unlike a typical team member review process in which a team member's work performance is evaluated by only the manager, which is an up-and-down approach, a 360 review takes into account feedback from peers and reporting staff—sometimes even customers and other people who interact with the team member.

Our 360 review process is meant to bring the entire organization up a level and is based on the biblical precepts offered by Solomon. Proverbs says, "As iron sharpens iron, so a friend sharpens a friend" (27:17) and "Faithful are the wounds of a friend" (27:6). Our 360 review process benefits our organization as it enables both managers and their team members to share about the real struggles they are facing. While we are honest and direct about each team member's core strengths (we focus on three strengths), we are also honest and direct about at least one area for improvement. We also listen carefully and prayerfully as each staff member gives feedback about his area for improvement. The goal is to make everyone better, not to simply give criticism. Together we're iron, and together we shore up each other's wounds (weaknesses).

As our company has grown and matured, I've observed how our 360 review process has helped us become a stronger organization in several important areas.

One of the most important benefits to a team member receiving 360-degree feedback is increased self-awareness. Each participant is given a complete report that includes three strengths and one area for improvement. This gives the team member better insight into his work and how it is perceived by others. This deeper understanding helps everyone to feel better about himself as there's less guesswork involved.

Another benefit is how we leverage each team member's individual strengths. Unearthing strengths is important for acknowledgment and also for personal improvement. Identifying strengths in a specific way allows a tailored plan for the future. A team member may exhibit strength in an area and when given additional development will excel even more. This is important for a team member's career growth and for the company's effectiveness.

Finally, it helps everyone to uncover blind spots, both on the part of the team member and the manager. When honest feedback is shared, everyone learns more about each other's work and expectations. This enables the team member to better understand his work in a way that he may not otherwise notice himself. Uncovering blind spots is important for continuous team member improvement. It also helps the manager to discover areas that might be missing in terms of how the

team member is being managed. Sometimes a team member underper-
forms simply because the manager is not using the most appropriate
management techniques.

While there are many good ways to review staff, I've learned that the
most effective way to review is with a biblical "loop" based on candidness,
forthrightness, and openness. This glorifies God as we are open to His
will and plans for our organization. In short, it works!

51

DONATIONS AS A MINISTRY

ONE OF THE great privileges you have as a CEO who believes in Jesus, and who's turned your company over to Him, is that you have the opportunity to bless others with your profits. I love that we donate 50 percent of our profits each year, and our entire team loves it as well. We all feel a sense of common purpose in being generous. My team tells me that they feel that our work is not only for our customers, or for the growth and success of our business, but also for the "least of those."

Who is the "least of those" whom Jesus calls our "least brother"? It's interesting that Jesus specifically points to the person considered the least, as opposed to a more general statement that includes all people. Why not say, "Whatever you do to others…?" But instead, Jesus pointed to the least brother. Perhaps Jesus means the weakest, the most gravely ill, the incapacitated, the widow or orphan, or the hungry and homeless. Jesus doesn't say specifically, but the Bible tells us much about who we should be generous with. For example, in Psalm 82:3, God commands us to "protect and care for orphans and widows." Also, Jesus shows great compassion for the sick. There are many other examples in scripture we can point to, so it's not hard to understand the types of people and communities the Bible commands us to help with the fruits of our labor.

But how to decide?

Eventually we made some decisions, and even now we'll sometimes decide to include other nonprofits in our giving. I'm often asked how we decided which organizations to donate to. Who do we consider to be "the least" in the eyes of Jesus?

This is a great question, and it did not come easily for us in the beginning. We thought about this, and we discussed it internally for quite some time. We decided to find and give generally to ten nonprofits. We initially thought it would be an easy decision to find ten groups, but it was not easy at all. There are thousands of charities, foundations, and other nonprofits to choose from that all do good work. Each has its own mission and outreach. Some are small while others are quite large. We wanted to choose wisely, and as we began to do our research, we did a lot of analysis. We even interviewed some nonprofits to find those that were making the greatest impact. But even then, it didn't necessarily matter if the organization was "effective." Some problems can be extremely difficult to solve, and you don't want to punish the charities working on those problems—otherwise, we'd only get charities working on easy problems.

After quite a bit of thinking, we decided to stop thinking and start praying for God to help us identify ten organizations. Then God worked an amazing miracle! A local news channel heard about our reputation for giving and did a feature story about our donation efforts. Soon the local story became national. This was quite exciting for my team and me. But nothing was as exciting as when afterwards, some nonprofit organizations reached out to us for help. Can you guess how many groups asked for a donation? Ten! We were astounded at how God answered our prayers. We had spent a great deal of time and effort analyzing this in our own heads, which only made it all the more complicated. Then when we asked God to help us, He provided the answer.

You might have guessed what I recommend you do with a portion of your profits. Bring it to God in prayer. While there are many good ways to give, only God knows the best way. I promise He will give you the answer, and you'll be grateful to know that your profits are blessing those that God wants to bless.

52

CONVICTION AND ACTION

I'M A STRONG believer in free markets, capitalism, and profits. We need an economy that allows each person to succeed through hard work and to lead a life of meaning and dignity. We need businesses, small and large, to grow and earn money. I believe the Bible supports that and would argue that entrepreneurs are God's gift to our country and to our world.

But I don't support large corporations (or small ones, for that matter) that put profits before people. One of the primary motivators for me to become an entrepreneur was a hatred of how some businesses are overly focused on the bottom line at the expense of their own people, even their own customers. They can become greedy. Proverbs says, "For he who is greedy for unjust gain brings trouble in his household" (Proverbs 15:27). Greed is a sin, and it can be easy for CEOs to be entrapped by it.

Almost all of the CEOs I know say they built their companies with people in mind, but the problem is that not all of them follow through, especially as their companies grow. No company survives without profits, of course. But if the bottom line or some other key indicator becomes the main priority, the consequences can be damaging. It will set the stage for internal resistance, lying, and other immoral behavior that can destroy your company. Hyper-focusing on one goal, particularly money, can cause team members to become so obsessed with it that they lose sight of other goals and values, such as treating customers and fellow team members with respect. This is an unhealthy and unbiblical way to run a company.

I believe that a healthy culture is as important as a healthy balance sheet. So we look out for the people who form the backbone of our company: our team members and our customers. As an entrepreneur and CEO, I was determined back when I started our company, and still am today, to place convictions over profits. I'm moved to think about and act on the convictions of my heart, as I understand God is moving me into actionable results. While I strive to lead a healthy and profitable business, it's not all about the money. In fact, we donate 50 percent of our profits to charities and organizations that closely align with our convictions.

What do I mean by convictions? A conviction is a strong belief about a truth. Biblical convictions are the doctrines we hold to be true and right, based on the Word and by the church throughout the centuries. Personal convictions are based upon scriptural truth and provide boundaries for us to live moral and ethical lives. They don't leave room for theological differences. They are not the gray areas. They are the black and white areas of our beliefs. Each of us may be convicted in a strong way to act on a certain thing, based on the Word.

As a company, we are convicted to use our profits to end human trafficking and to help the poor, particularly poor children in orphanages. We do so because the Bible tells us to do so: "Speak up for those who cannot speak for themselves, for the rights of all who are destitute. Speak up and judge fairly; defend the rights of the poor and needy" (Proverbs 31:8–9). Many years ago, I was convicted by the Holy Spirit to use our company as a means to speak up for those who cannot speak for themselves. So a part of our core values is to put people first, not profits, and we do this with actionable results. We literally give away some of our profits to organizations that fight human trafficking and poverty.

There's no greater feeling that knowing all of our hard work pays dividends, not in our bank accounts or wallets, but in impacting lives for the Gospel. Our convictions are more than about bottom-line profits but bottom-line lives. Our efforts to create and sell products literally save lives! Why? Because we have convictions, based on the Word of God, that move us to use our business savvy and skills for the sake of the Gospel. This is the ultimate dividend!

ENDNOTES

[1] https://www.forbes.com/sites/benjaminlaker/2021/04/23/culture-is-a-companys-single-most-powerful-advantage-heres-why/?sh=3fe9145c679e

[2] https://www.inc.com/scott-mautz/jeff-bezos-says-this-is-single-biggest-sign-that-someone-is-intelligent-its-counterintuitive.html

[3] https://www.fastcompany.com/90465402/how-to-actually-create-a-fun-company-culture

[4] https://www.forbes.com/sites/peterhigh/2019/11/25/half-of-all-meetings-are-a-waste-of-timeheres-how-to-improve-them/?sh=d2f-959d2ea9e

[5] https://online.hbs.edu/blog/post/why-is-strategic-planning-important

[6] https://visionedgemarketing.com/developing-pricing-model/

[7] https://www.forbes.com/sites/markhall/2018/06/25/how-ceo-spend-time/?sh=325aceb34728

[8] https://www.superoffice.com/blog/customer-experience-statistics/

CPSIA information can be obtained
at www.ICGtesting.com
Printed in the USA
LVHW100753180422
716359LV00003B/16